Political Thinking

The Perennial Questions

Political Thinking

The Perennial Questions

Second Edition

Glenn Tinder

University of Massachusetts, Boston

LITTLE, BROWN AND COMPANY   Boston

SEVENTH PRINTING

Published simultaneously in Canada
by Little, Brown & Company (Canada) Limited

Printed in the United States of America

To Galen,
son and independent thinker

Preface

The guiding idea in the first edition of *Political Thinking* —
that political theory and politics in general can advantageously
be studied by paying far more attention than is customary to
the great questions underlying the theory and practice of government — is unchanged in the present edition. My purpose in
writing a second edition was not to introduce radical changes,
but to strengthen the first edition. I believe that the present
edition is at once more solid and more readable. Adding substance are several new questions, although the total number of
questions remains the same. Most of these new questions appear in chapters 6 and 7 (the chapters on the ends of power and
on historical change), both of which have been completely re-
structured. The discussions have been reinforced at numerous
points. Although in their general purport the questions are
largely unchanged, they have in many instances been rephrased
in order that they might be simpler and more direct. The style
and content of all material carried over from the first edition
has been carefully reconsidered.

I hope, then, that nothing valuable in the first edition has
been lost, and that this is a weightier and more usable book. If
this hope is justified, some credit belongs to political scientists
who have used the book in their classes, and who, with their
praise, encouraged me to work further on the book and, with
their criticisms, helped me to determine where work was needed.

Contents

Contents

CHAPTER 4

Power   73

CHAPTER 5

Restraints on Power   101

CHAPTER 6

The Ends of Power   127

Contents

Political
Thinking

The Perennial Questions

Introduction

Political Thinking may prove to be a rather difficult and trying book for some readers — and not necessarily for readers who are careless and superficial in their reading, either. It may be difficult and trying for the best readers because it is made up wholly of questions and contains no answers. Not only do I give no indication as to the answers I accept; sometimes I am as unsure of them as the reader is likely to be. Hence the book has none of the satisfying finality that is characteristic of most books.

This comment is a forewarning but not an apology; the primary intent of the book requires that the reader be denied any positions of repose. My purpose is to provide an introduction to political thinking; I have tried to do this, however, not by presenting the great political philosophies of the past but rather by impelling the reader to engage in the activity of thinking himself. This end has necessitated asking questions but withholding answers.

It has been said that anyone who makes people believe that they are thinking will be loved by them, whereas anyone who actually makes them think will be hated. If so, then some degree of exasperation on the part of the reader (although I have tried not to cause more exasperation than is intellectually fruitful) will be a sign of the book's success.

Perhaps too much is said in universities about how "exciting" it is to think. Thinking undoubtedly has its excitements and satisfactions, but these feelings do not disclose its general character, and there is something very much wrong with the idea they should. We do not think in order to have fun but because life is troubling and problematic. We think because we are compelled to. And while thinking occasionally brings exciting discoveries, the periods in between these discoveries are likely to place heavy demands not only on the thinker's energies but on his patience as well. When thinking, we should not need to tell ourselves that it is an exhilarating experience; it should be enough to realize that we are behaving with the seriousness, the rationality, and the self-discipline that the human situation requires of us.

Such gravity is particularly applicable to *political* thinking in so tragic an age as the twentieth century. Should one expect to find it altogether enjoyable to ponder the kind of dilemmas that have within recent decades cost uncounted millions of lives?

Thus the following pages are not supposed to be easy or uplifting. They are supposed, rather, to introduce the reader to the trials of political thinking in an age of turmoil and doubt.

Once he has gotten onto the high seas of thought, however, a reader may feel that more instruction than is to be found in this book should have been given on navigating and remaining afloat. How does one go about thinking? I shall offer a few suggestions in this foreword. Help of this kind, however, is necessarily of limited value. Much of the trying and demanding nature of thought results from the impossibility of conducting it according to teachable techniques. Much is said about "teaching students to think." But a teacher can do little more than offer encouragement and criticism. The appearance of an idea is a mysterious occurrence, and it is doubtful that anyone does, or ever will, understand just how it comes about.

But a student can *learn* to think. The reason for saying that he cannot be *taught* to think is to focus at the outset on the dependence of the entire process on the student's own solitary efforts. It is both the glory and the burden of thought that it is an exceedingly personal undertaking. The solitude of the

mature thinker must be entered into immediately by the beginner. As the mature thinker thinks all alone, the beginner
must *learn* to think all alone. Occasionally one may receive a
gift of encouragement or useful criticism, but nothing is decided by these gifts. Everything depends on the capacity for
solitary effort.

It follows that little instruction in the art of thinking can be
offered here beyond some fragmentary suggestions such as
these:

1. Do not try to arrive at ideas that no one has ever thought
of before. Not many of even the greatest thinkers have done
that. The aim of thinking is to discover ideas that pull together
one's world, and thus one's being, not to give birth to un-
precedented conceptions. An idea is your own if it has grown
by your own efforts and is rooted in your own emotions and
experience, even though you may have received the seeds from
someone else and even though the idea may be very much like
ideas held by many others.

2. Be open. Ideas cannot be deliberately produced like industrial products. They appear uncommanded, they "occur,"
as we recognize when we say, "It occurred to me that . . . ."
Hence one places himself in a fundamentally wrong relationship with ideas if he conceives of himself as controlling their
appearance. He can only be open to them.

3. Do not hurry. Initial efforts to think about a problem are
often completely frustrating. They may best be regarded as a
tilling of the ground; time is required before anything can be
expected to grow.

4. Make plenty of notes. It is easier to do work with your
mind if you are doing some corresponding work with your
hands. It is often helpful to make notes on large pads where
there is room for sketching out patterns of ideas. It can also
be helpful to make notes on cards and then to cut up the cards
so that each idea is on a small section of card. These can then
be laid out on a desk and rearranged. Often this process suggests new connections.

5. Beware of substituting reading for thinking. Reading
about the thoughts of others is not the same as having thoughts
of your own. To be sure, one who engages in thinking needs

some acquaintance with the thoughts of others. The great thinkers inspire, provoke, confirm, and in other ways help one to do his own thinking. But one who is going to think must at some point lay down the book and strike out on his own.

I have a final suggestion that I do not number with the five above because it must take the form, not of a briefly stated "tip" but of a somewhat extended comment on the structure of political thought.

Most political ideas, perhaps in the last analysis all of them, are grounded on some particular conception of man. The conservative idea that political authority should be strong and highly centralized, for example, is apt to be based on a conception of man as selfish and competitive; the liberal notion that extensive social changes can ordinarily be brought about peacefully arises from the premise that human beings are for the most part reasonable. These examples are very simple, and in an actual political philosophy the relations between the underlying conception of man and the superstructure of political ideas may be far more complex; they do, however, illustrate, the general structure which is implicitly or explicitly present in almost every political theory.

What is the bearing of this observation on the question as to how one should go about thinking? Simply this: One is apt to find that his mind is clarified and stimulated through articulating this structure in his own thought. In the course of political thinking one should occasionally pause to ask himself how he envisions man and what implications his vision of man has for his political ideas.

One may feel that to ask in this way about the nature of man is to face a mystery even darker than those encountered on the level of political reflection. There are, however, two overriding issues in this area, despite the infinite complexities of human nature; one may initiate the process of thought by trying to respond to these issues. One issue concerns the extent and origins of evil in man: Is man deeply and incurably evil, or is evil a superficial and removable aspect of his character? The second issue — less universally recognized nowadays than the first — concerns the import of death: Is an individual totally extinguished when he dies? Does the term "salvation" correspond to anything that may actually happen?

4

One's response to the first issue will very largely determine his ideas on such matters as how much freedom man should have, to what extent historical progress is possible, and the degree of violence necessary to bring about change. One's response to the second issue decides in a general way his whole conception of the purpose of life. One who believes that death is complete extinction must somehow call on men (using Nietzsche's words) to "be true to the earth," for example, whereas one who does not believe that death is extinction must see earthly politics as significant only insofar as it helps or hinders man in working out his relations with a transcendent entity.

Perhaps it is in order to say here that these ethical and metaphysical areas contain many pitfalls and surprises and that one should be wary both of offhand answers and of offhand inferences from his anwers.

For example, it is often assumed today that affirming the goodness of man, if an error, is a generous and harmless error. Hence political discussions are often punctuated with complacent expressions of trust in human nature. But this trust can have some paradoxical results. If man is fundamentally good, then how does there happen to be so much evil in human affairs? It is hard to avoid concluding that it must be because some people are exceptions to the general human norm. Thus Communists have tended to blame all of the evil in the world on capitalists, and vice versa. It is apparent how sinister a line of thought this is, for the next step is deciding that to free the human race from evil it is necessary only to eradicate the few who are the sources of this evil. Through so natural a logic as this a benign and generous judgment becomes murderous.

On the other hand, one should not lightly judge man to be evil, for if I believe that man is evil, how can I avoid having my life dominated by hatred and by hopelessness?

As for the issue of death, here too there are pitfalls. It has often been noted that to deny the finality of death can imperil man's freedom. This is simply because such a denial can only be based on religious faith and religious faith readily takes the form of a dogma forcibly imposed on everyone.

It does not follow, however, that simply accepting the finality of death is safe and sets up no dangerous reverberations in the area of political thought. For example, it is doubtful whether the idea that every individual is an end in himself, a repository of unique dignity, would ever have arisen apart from the idea that every individual is immortal. The idea of personal immortality disentangled the individual from natural realities and set him above the whole natural world. That is why he could not be regarded as a mere means but had to be regarded as an end. If he is not immortal, however, he tends to sink back into nature and in some circumstances to be regarded, like any other natural being, as a means rather than an end.

The reader is apt to feel that he cannot possibly decide issues so vast. And of course he cannot, if deciding them means finding answers which are exact and sure, answers which are never altered and never doubted. But it should be noted that these vast issues do not concern something far away but rather the most immediate and intimate of realities — one's own self. Is one not in a position at least to hazard some guesses concerning the nature and destiny of persons, when he is a person himself? And can one live without making some assumptions concerning these matters? And if one is to make some assumptions, is it not just as well to bring them into the open and let reason examine them?

But how is one to judge the truth of his ideas? This question can be asked not only about ideas concerning man but about political ideas in general. How can one test the validity of an idea that has occurred to him and appeals to him and that he has perhaps shaped and polished?

There are some standard and well-known tests: The idea must be consistent with other ideas one holds at the same time, and it should explain, or at the very least be compatible with, all established, relevant facts. But even the most conscientious and dispassionate application of these criteria is not apt to carry one very far. It can never, in the field of political theory, lead to proof; it probably will not lead to life and meaning. A set of ideas may be internally consistent and compatible with all known facts and still be dead and useless. Hence in learning to identify the truth one needs to look beyond these standard criteria — but not, I suggest, toward another criterion so much as toward the ideal of wholeness and integration that is implicit in the standard criteria.

In the last analysis, an idea is living and important only so far as it brings one into relationship with himself and with reality, so far as it "pulls things together." What is implied by the standards of logical consistency and factual accuracy is that nothing must be suppressed and nothing ignored. An idea has the function of extending and integrating relationships. Hence, an idea that calls on one to ignore things that he knows or deeply believes to be true must be judged false or at least inadequate; it has a disintegrating effect on his experience and being. A true idea is one that makes for inclusiveness and unity.

Feeling necessarily has a great part in searching for the truth. Much that must be pulled together does not have the definite and conscious form of a fact or an idea. A great idea is one that symbolizes and unifies not only facts and beliefs that are clearly present to consciousness but also intuitions and impulses that have not been focused upon and given form. It is the idea that does this that is "exciting." This may seem an invitation to believe whatever is pleasant or interesting. It must therefore be added that thinking tries one's depth and honesty. One is thinking deeply and well when he acknowledges and draws together into a single and coherent pattern all that emerges from his experience and emotions; his search must be without sentimentality or carelessness or fear.

As for the best way of using the present volume, the same kind of reading that is customary for most other books — that is, without long pauses for reflection, discussion, and writing — should prove of some value. Although the questions are posed without being resolved, they are linked together in a way that makes them a wandering pathway over the terrain of political thought. Through an ordinary reading one should gain some sense of the intellectual state in which political thinking originates.

This book is designed, however, not just to be read but to be used — through discussion, through writing, and through prolonged reflection. The questions are set forth not simply to inform readers concerning the dilemmas of others but to draw them into dilemmas of their own. This will happen only if, in addition to reading the book as a whole, one dwells on at least a few of the questions and tries to answer them. The questions are clearly stated, separated, and numbered to facilitate their being used in such ways.

While I believe that reflection on politics is an end in itself, I should add that this book may, in my opinion, contribute to the study of the history of political theory. Really to understand the great thinkers requires getting some sense of the interior of their minds, and doing this depends on entering in some measure into the doubts and anxieties that provoked them to thought. Only a rare and profound intellectual sympathy — or empathy — brought to bear in the analysis of a particular thinker can make this possible. What *Political Thinking* can do, I think, is to help readers gain a vantage point from which such sympathy, gained from their own insight, or from a teacher or biographer, will become possible.

A final point that I would like particularly to emphasize is that a reader's formulation of new questions is no less in the spirit of the book than his formulation of answers to the questions I have asked. There can be no final and definitive set of questions. The most that can be claimed for this book is that it covers in a general way the whole area of political thought; I scarcely need to say that I do not see it as asking every important question or as asking the questions it does ask in the best possible way. Thus readers who find themselves rephrasing some of the questions or asking questions other than those included in the book should proceed with clear consciences. The aim of the book is to engage the reader in intellectual movement, and the original source of all such movement is asking questions.

Why Engage in Political Thinking?

One reason for asking this question is that thinking is a peculiarly arduous and discouraging undertaking. Of course, it is often remarked that thinking is hard work. However, one who enters fully into the process of questioning set forth in the following chapters will discover that the difficulties of thinking are far more subtle and exasperating than those of mere hard work. He is apt to find, for example, that the effort of thought at first is completely fruitless; to admit uncertainty, as one must in order to think, may seem to leave one in a kind of void with no horizons in the distance and no solid ground underneath. Further, anyone who tries to think will find himself annoyingly subject to daydreaming and persistently inclined to think about other things than the question before him. Finally, he will discover that the products of thought often are intangible and fleeting. Ideas that have taken hours to develop may evaporate owing to a few remarks by a sophisticated friend.

A thinking person is exceedingly vulnerable. He must appear before others, not behind the armor and shield of books he has read and of ideas formulated by others but in the nakedness of his own thoughts and doubts.

Nor are the long-range results that come from this precarious and nervewracking effort apt to be obviously and unarguably good. It is not manifest that thinking is the way to moral elevation, to happiness, or even to wisdom. More than two thousand years of philosophical doubt and disagreement have proven that it is not the way to unshakable and enduring knowledge. Undoubtedly something tells many of us that it would be ignoble deliberately to refrain from thinking. But this monitor is not heard by everyone; it was not heard, for example, by as great a writer as Rousseau, who believed that through thinking one alienates himself from reality and from his own being.

Contemporary American culture is apt to reinforce one's natural reluctance to think. Certainly verbal tributes are frequently paid to goals like "making people stop and think." But Americans today do not seem to assign much importance to thought that is of philosophic breadth and seriousness. One can verify this conclusion by noting how rarely a truly philosophical work is found on the lists of best-selling books. The political books that become widely known are mostly factual and hortatory tracts concerning urgent problems such as poverty and racial tension. One of the most gifted contemporary thinkers, Hannah Arendt, is famous primarily for a topical and relatively unimportant book about Eichmann and the Nazi death camps; her major work of political thought, *The Human Condition,* is little known. As for political scientists, who might seem to have a special responsibility for political thinking, the behavioralism that is currently ascendant among them is often overtly antiphilosophical.

Of course, any society probably has an inherent bias against original thought. Social order depends heavily on tradition and habit, and these are apt to be weakened by real thinking. The execution of Socrates in Athens exemplifies this antagonism. Nevertheless, I suggest that today in America two forces, both stronger than they have been in many times and places, intensify the normal antiphilosophical cast of society and deepen the reluctance of individuals to subject themselves to the uneasiness and labor of thought.

One of these forces is a strong liking for action. Americans have probably always been biased toward action, which our

environment both necessitated and rewarded. Today the traditional American inclination to resort to action has been reinforced by the multitude and gravity of the problems confront-
ing us — problems such as urban disintegration and persisting
racial injustice. Thus politically conscious Americans at present are intensely preoccupied with all of the things that demand doing and are confident of man's power to do these
things successfully. This dynamic spirit is in many ways advantageous; despondency is avoided and often great tasks are
accomplished. But it makes people impatient with reflection
and disinclined to entertain questions that do not have an immediate practical urgency. They seek programs of action.

The other antiphilosophical force that seems particularly
strong in present-day America is a thirst for facts, which, at
least partially, is a result of the bias toward action. Most
Americans want to know what is actually going on — in the
schools, in the ghettos, in the nonindustrial countries. If asked
whether human beings are essentially estranged (the first
question that will be considered in the following pages), they
are apt to inquire what that has to do with the deterioration of
the inner city or the poverty of Africa and Asia — and not as
though they really are inquiring but rather as though they are
dismissing the question as irrelevant. The thirst for facts is not,
of course, any more inherently reprehensible than is the bias
toward action. Facts can be verified and often can be put to
practical use, which is more than can be said for most philosophical theories. But perhaps philosophical theories are important in other ways. This possibility is not likely to be of
much interest to those who are avid for information.

In sum, the paths of thought are not altogether inviting.
Following them leads inevitably to toil and insecurity but not
necessarily to solid answers or inner rest. Also, for Americans,
thinking is contrary to their culture, which presses on them
continually the prior urgency of acting and of gaining reliable
information.

Then why — to recur to the title of this chapter — engage in
political thinking?

For one thing, some questions cannot be answered by any
other means. For example, when does one have the right to

disobey the government? Can a government legitimately break moral laws if the welfare of the nation seems to require it? Should all social and economic inequalities be abolished? Questions of this kind cannot be answered without thought. Information bearing on them may come from social sciences, from personal experience, from history, and from other sources. But only thought can determine what information is truly relevant and then use it in answering the questions.

But — to speak for many Americans — must such questions be answered? Would we not be better off concentrating on the concrete problems at hand? The answer to both questions can be found in the principle that to adopt any attitude at all toward reality, even one of concentrating on practical matters and spurning philosophical reflection, is at least implicitly to adopt a philosophical position. The very idea that practical problems should have priority over philosophical problems is philosophical; it is philosophical because it can be formulated and defended only through philosophical reflection. Hence it can be said that questions of the kind Americans are inclined impatiently to dismiss are imposed on us by our life. We have no choice as to whether to answer them. Our only alternative is answering them reflectively and with care, or answering them thoughtlessly and irresponsibly.

To put the matter in another way, only through ideas can we discern and enter fully into relations with reality. An idea is a kind of light; many of the great political ideas have the power of illuminating not only what is but what ought to be. If it were not for these ideas, man's collective life would be immersed in darkness.

Thus, for example, it is apparent to most of us that Nazism was fundamentally wrong. This would not be apparent, however, were it not for ideas like the dignity of law and the evil of tyranny; and these are not innate ideas of the human mind but were formed by reflective men, such as Aristotle, Cicero, and Locke. As another example, it is plain to many of us today that the segregated and inferior position of black people in America is unjust. But why is this so plain? Comparable arrangements have prevailed in many societies for thousands of years and have been taken for granted by most of the inhabitants of those societies; one can cite, as an example, Aristotle's casual acceptance of slavery. The light in which we view America's racial situation comes from the idea of equality — an idea we probably would not possess had it not been for thinkers such as Locke, Rousseau, and Marx. Perhaps eight or ten ideas — these not innate in the human mind, but rather products of reflection — are the lanterns of political civilization; they enable us to discern and judge the realities of collective life.

Both the action and the facts prized today in American culture presuppose ideas and the thinking that forms them. As for action, in order to act intelligently we must have ends we are seeking to effect. What are ends, however, but ideas of a certain kind — ideas concerning some desirable state of affairs? For example, during the last two centuries men have often protested and rebelled in order to gain self-government. But for several millennia men acquiesced unprotestingly most of the time in the rule of highly exclusive elites. Thus the demand for self-government does not arise from human nature; it is called forth by an idea. Activist Americans, impatient of thought, stand on a groundwork of ideas that has been built by reflection. If that groundwork were removed, they and all of their plans would fall into a barbaric void where intelligent action would have no place.

Something similar can be said also of the thirst for facts. This thirst is not satisfied by indiscriminately gathering in every fact that happens to be noticed. Such research would only create a chaos of insignificant and unrelated atoms of information. Indeed, without ideas concerning both what is real and what is significant, it is doubtful that any such thing as a fact could be discovered, for facts do not just lie about like pebbles; their very existence depends on the power of mind to distinguish and relate. An interest in facts that deserves any respect at all is an interest in organized and significant knowledge, which cannot be available where there are no ideas. Consider, for example, the amount of knowledge we possess concerning poverty and the culture surrounding it. Can anyone think that we would possess this knowledge if the ideas of Marx and other socialists and social reformers had not inspired and directed its accumulation?

Of course, only a few great thinkers create the ideas that

illuminate reality and thus guide action and research. But the fact that the most influential thinking is done by the few does not mean that all the others need not think at all. For one thing, the great thinkers do not agree. They offer different and often mutually contradictory ideas. How can one decide which ideas to accept without doing some thinking on his own?

Further, even if one were willing to commit himself to certain ideas instinctively and uncritically, he probably could not understand them without having experienced some of the labor and doubt that have gone into creating them. What is meant, for instance, by the idea that men are equal? Clearly they are not equal in any measurable quality such as intelligence or health or emotional balance. One may say that they are equal only in their rights before the law. But why should they be accorded equal rights before the law if they are in no respect equal in fact? The question need not be pursued. It is plain that for someone who has never reflected on the matter, the concept of equality can hardly have any intelligible content.

Thus, despite the emphasis in this book on questions rather than answers, my first response to the query, "Why engage in political thinking?" is that one does so for the sake of answers that cannot be reached in any other way.

This response, however, ignores one of the weightiest and oldest objections to philosophical thought about politics or any other subject — that the ideas it reaches must always be undemonstrable and uncertain. It follows that to engage in thinking is to entertain doubts that can never, through thought, be wholly overcome.

This objection seems sound. Few, if any, of the main political ideas held by a typical American or European at the present time can be proven; most of them can be severely shaken. Substantial arguments, for example, can be brought against even so seemingly solid an idea as the rule of law. As Plato argued, that rule inhibits full application of intelligence to social problems; further, in times of bitterness and disorder, such as those we live in, it is a rule that may restrict the initiative and energy of the police and thus may enhance the difficulty of protecting property and persons. The reader will perhaps think of answers to these arguments, but he will not think of any that conclusively refute them. Every important idea is attended by some inseparable counter-ideas; the idea of freedom, for example, calls to mind and can never altogether destroy or subordinate to itself the idea of authority. In reaching the "answers" referred to above, a number of counter-ideas must be more or less subdued; but they are apt to prove recurrently troublesome and refractory to one who refuses to turn his "answers" into ironclad dogmas.

The history of political thought shows how doubt continually pursues thought and frequently overtakes it. There is no more agreement concerning political truth now than there was twenty-five hundred years ago, when political thinking began. There may well be less.

This divergence of opinion sharpens our original question. Why engage in inquiry of a kind that can only lead to uncertain and disputable conclusions?

Here we have an exceedingly important question, for the issue it brings before us is whether it is worthwhile trying to reason about the ultimate ends and the fundamental assumptions governing our lives in common. This, after all, is the business of political thinking. Clearly, one's position on this issue will have a great deal to do with his whole conception of how society should be organized. At the same time, the question is very difficult. Like the other questions with which political thinking deals, this one, having to do with the value of political thinking itself, has no incontrovertible answer.

It seems appropriate, therefore, to suggest answers that will enable us to move into the area of the perennial questions with some confidence that we are not wasting our time. But these answers will be provisional, for we shall return to the whole issue in the Epilogue, after the reader has gained experience in the task of reflection. The following are three provisional answers.

First, while political ideas and political philosophies contain subjective elements (like a work of art, a political philosophy is emphatically and thoroughly the creation of a particular person, lacking the impersonal authority of a body of scientific laws), they are not wholly subjective. Very simply, one cannot believe whatever he chooses. One must conform to the evidence and to the rules of logical consistency. Granted, none of the great ideas or philosophies is demonstrably true. But it would be easy to formulate an idea or a philosophy that is demonstrably false, either because it is contrary to unchallengeable factual data or because it is internally contradictory. The uncertainty of political ideas should not be exaggerated.

The second reason for believing that political speculation is not vain, although its results are unavoidably open to doubt, is implicit in what has been said about the need for ideas that can only be reached through thought. However disputable the conclusions of thought may be, we cannot live in a civilized fashion without them. It may seem unsatisfactory that our ideas are so vulnerable to doubt; but it is far better to have doubtful ideas than to have none at all. The former state is uncomfortable but civilized, the latter barbarous.

Finally, it is worth engaging in inquiry of a kind that can never conquer doubt simply for the value inherent in the act of inquiry itself. Through thinking, I suggest, one gains a humanity that is not available in any other way. What we are threatened with by the present passion for action and for facts, even though this passion often expresses a strong civic conscience, is a brutalization that is inseparable from thoughtlessness.

How is humanity gained through thought?

First of all, by questioning and reflecting one realizes his own being, in its freedom and distinctness. "All deep, earnest thinking," Herman Melville wrote, "is but the intrepid effort of the soul to keep the open independence of her sea." He added, speaking again of the soul or the self, that "the wildest winds of heaven and earth conspire to cast her on the treacherous, slavish shore." [1] Today we may interpret the "treacherous, slavish shore" as a symbol of some of the vast, impersonal realities that seem to be suffocating the individual: ideology, for example, or bureaucratic routine or mass opinion. To think is to stand apart; it is to affirm one's own irreducible reality.

---

[1] Herman Melville, *Moby Dick, or The Whale* (New York: The Modern Library, 1930), p. 153.

Those who regard political thinking as futile, owing to its inconclusiveness, should be reminded that the totalitarian dictators of the twentieth century have done everything possible to stifle such thinking. One reason for this repression is certainly that political thinking expresses and nurtures free personality. It may be worthwhile, also, to note the difference in capacity for thought between the human and the subhuman. Is it not significant that these supposedly futile questions cannot be raised by rocks or trees or dogs, but only by human beings?

Further, through thinking one not only affirms his own distinct being; he also defines it. Thinking is a summoning of the self. When one reflects on a problem of philosophical scope, he must call into consciousness and test and relate his strongest impressions and convictions. He must think back on all he has read and ask how much of it is reliable and important and has bearing on the question at hand. He also must consult his own past and ask what he has experienced and felt that should be taken into account. In ways such as these, through thinking one shapes his personal being. This aspect of thinking implies that the subjective quality of thought, with its correspondingly objective uncertainty, is not altogether a drawback. Such subjectivity deprives philosophy of the universally compelling power of scientific law; but it enables reflection to play a part in the establishment of personal identity that scientific research cannot play.

Finally, thought enhances one's humanity by requiring openness to others. If all serious and candid reflection is an admission that one may be mistaken, it is, by the same token, an admission that others may be right. In this sense, thinking is a communal state; here one breaks down the walls of his own certitude and enters into relation with the ideas of others. Undoubtedly, strong convictions have had a part in the development of political philosophies; perhaps everyone needs convictions of some kind. On the other hand, convictions have certainly done much harm; they have made human beings hard and closed, thus dividing them from one another. So far as one thinks, he questions his convictions and thus overcomes the contempt people always tend to feel for parties, nations, and eras with convictions counter to their own. Thus, if by thinking one distinguishes himself from others in their conformity and thoughtlessness, by the same act he joins them in their pitiful uncertainty.

Some philosophers have held that thinking is a pathway not only to selfhood and community but also to consciousness of transcendence or God. For atheists and agnostics, of course, if this were so, then thinking would be a pathway to illusions and would certainly not be a way of gaining humanity. Even many believers will be surprised, and perhaps offended, by the idea that an activity destructive of certainty and leading to no definite and undeniable conclusions can bring one into contact with God. Is not faith or religious consciousness, after all, a state of absolute certainty in which all doubts and questions are definitively set aside? Some thinkers of great stature have said that it is not.[2] Human certainties, according to these thinkers, are idols, and God cannot be contained in any of man's dogmas.

Those who see things in this way are apt to hold that instilling religious openness and awareness is one of the main ways in which thinking contributes to our humanity. According to this view there is no antagonism between God and creative personal being, but rather a mysterious unity. Thus the great German philosopher, Karl Jaspers (1883–1969), asserted flatly that "freedom and God are inseparable." And he added, in one of his typically difficult but interesting utterances: "Where I am authentically myself, I am certain that I am not through myself. The highest freedom is experienced in freedom from the world, and this freedom is a profound bond with transcendence."[3]

This issue, too, will be touched upon again in the Epilogue.

Meanwhile, perhaps we can reflect on some of the great questions of political thought with a sense that we are doing

---

[2] Martin Buber, Gabriel Marcel, and Karl Jaspers, all of whom lived and wrote in the twentieth century, are probably the major thinkers who have taken this position.

[3] Karl Jaspers, *Way to Wisdom: An Introduction to Philosophy*, translated by Ralph Manheim (New Haven: Yale University Press, 1951), p. 45.

something worthwhile in spite of our inability to reach impregnable conclusions. If there is any validity in the views just outlined, then one can hope to reach ideas that are tentative, but not at all arbitrary or capricious, and are of the kind on which the viability of civilization depends. One can hope also to deepen his consciousness of himself, of others, and perhaps of transcendence.

Today we possess awesome powers of action, as manifest in our command of nuclear energy, our penetration into space, and our industrial productivity. We also possess highly developed skills in accumulating and interpreting facts, as is dramatically evident in the scope and refinement of the physical sciences and in the vast amount of data accumulated in the social sciences. But it is doubtful that we possess wisdom. Our lives are therefore carried on under an ineffaceable question: Can we make our powers of action and our skills in research serve any valid ultimate purpose? The widespread fear that we may destroy civilization or even all of life, through nuclear war, shows how far we are from being able confidently to give an affirmative answer to this unassuming little question.

I suggest that the wisdom demanded by our powers of action and research does not lie in knowing beyond all doubt but in a certain kind of not-knowing — in the uncertainty that expresses both independent selfhood and openness to others. One has a strong yearning for absolute assurance as to what is true and right; one feels his whole identity shaken when his assurance is shaken. But the identity thus imperiled is false. It depends on certitude rather than on thought. This book is based on the premise that man in his finitude and freedom is a thinking being. Hence, one who learns to consider questions with clarity and determination and an open mind gains something that is irreducible to knowledge — the wisdom and poise of humane uncertainty.

Estrangement and Unity

The word estrangement is used here to signify every kind of disunity among human beings. War among nations, conflict among classes, and personal alienation, all are manifestations of estrangement; hatred, indifference, and loneliness are emotions of estrangement.

If there were no estrangement, there would be no politics. Webster's Dictionary specifies, as an antonym of "estrange," the verb "reconcile." Following this lead, it may be said that politics is the art of reconciliation and that the need for this art always arises from some kind of estrangement. When the leaders of one nation covet territory held by another nation or when one class is resentful of hardships not borne by other classes, demands are placed on political leadership. Of course, not every kind of estrangement necessarily gives rise to political demands; it is not yet clear, for example, whether the personal alienation that seems to be so acutely felt in advanced industrial societies at the present time constitutes in any way a political problem. The point is, however, that while not every situation of estrangement produces political problems, all political problems are rooted in situations involving estrangement.

If estrangement is the fundamental condition of politics, it is the fundamental condition also of political thinking. If men were not estranged, whether in quiet loneliness or in active conflict, political thinking would not occur. We are impelled to ask about the ultimate forces and standards governing human relations only when those relations are strained and destroyed. Thus the greatest achievements of political thought have for the most part been responses to social disintegration. *The Republic* of Plato can be read as a meditation on the Peloponnesian War, in which the Greek cities not only fought one another for several decades but were inwardly torn by ferocious factional conflicts; *The City of God* by Saint Augustine is an explicit commentary on the fall of the Roman Empire; Thomas Hobbes's *Leviathan* was called forth by the civil wars of seventeenth-century England; and it was the degeneration of the *ancien régime*, as manifest in the artificiality and loneliness of Parisian intellectual life and the autocracy of royal officials, that inspired the essays of Rousseau.

Hence, we must begin our questioning by trying to probe the nature of estrangement — by inquiring, for example, to what extent it is inherent in the very nature of man and by what means and to what extent it can be counteracted or overcome.

The most fundamental question about estrangement concerns its ultimate origin. Do such conditions as loneliness and conflict derive from the universal and unchangeable nature of man, so that as long as the human species endures men will be estranged from one another? Or is estrangement owing to circumstances that can be altered or of human characteristics that can be eliminated without destroying anything essentially human?

1

Are human beings estranged in essence?

Today this question presses on us from various sides, although we do not often recognize it. For example, can we hope ever to achieve harmony and understanding among all the nations of the world? If human beings are not estranged in essence, perhaps we can. However, if they are thus estranged — if, for example, man has ineradicable aggressive impulses — a wise statesman will not aim at anything so far-reaching as global understanding and unity. If human nature is such that the deepest satisfactions are experienced in war and combat, then there is little use in dreaming of universal concord; it will be an accomplishment if our hatreds can remain moderate and our wars confined to limited areas and to the less destructive weapons.

The importance of this question is exemplified also in the conflict of races. Can we hope ever to achieve full racial integration? Certainly we can if racial hostility is not an expression of the human essence. But perhaps man is essentially an uneasy and suspicious creature who is "put off" even by superficial differences in other men. If that is so, even though we may be deeply convinced that racial differences are trivial and nonessential, we probably should not strive for racial integration; in these circumstances, absence of conflict, uniform justice, and decent conditions of life for everyone would be sensible and sufficiently elevated aims.

As Fascism shows, it is possible to envision man in a way that invalidates even the goal of reducing conflict. War and racial domination, given a certain conception of man, may be the highest ideals.

The question of whether men are essentially estranged also presses on us through the alienation pervading contemporary middle-class life. Many people today apparently feel that although their lives are superficially harmonious and comfortable, they lack relationships that are substantial and significant. Such conditions as the disintegration of families and the mobility entailed by many jobs tend to make all personal links tenuous and impermanent. But would those who bewail the lack of community find, if once they could enter into a community, that it is actually of little value or is even positively undesirable? Is defiant individuality perhaps a much greater value, and should we learn to cherish the solitude so often imposed on us rather than merely to endure it? Community is everywhere extolled. But is privacy perhaps a far greater good? Such questions can be answered only by determining whether human beings are estranged in essence.

There are always more than two opposite answers to fundamental questions. However, in order to delineate sharply and concisely the issues presented, it will sometimes be convenient to discuss only the polar positions. This procedure will be followed in discussing the present question.

No other philosopher has so ably and pungently argued that men are essentially estranged as Thomas Hobbes (1588–1679). The natural condition of man, Hobbes maintained, is one of war, a war "of every man, against every man." Where there is no strong central government "to over-awe them all," then "men have no pleasure, but on the contrary a great deal of grief, in keeping company." Life in such a state, as Hobbes asserted in one of the most famous phrases in political literature, must be "solitary, poor, nasty, brutish, and short." [1]

There are, so to speak, two levels of estrangement in Hobbes's philosophy. One level is psychological. Men are estranged simply because they are essentially egotistical. Each person is concerned above all with the preservation of his own life; secondarily, he seeks such things as wealth and prestige. None of these benefits can be gained without power. Thus Hobbes attributed to man "a perpetual and restless desire of power after power, that ceaseth only in death." [2] A man cares nothing about others except as they can help him or hinder him in reaching his own private goals. Such self-centeredness is not perverse; it is man's true nature. Nor is it avoidable. To be human is to be concerned exclusively with personal interests and personal power.

Beneath the psychological level of estrangement is what can be called the "ontological" level. Ontology is the science of being in general, and the word "ontological" is intended here to refer to Hobbes's conception of the nature of being. Hobbes is ordinarily, and accurately, considered a materialist. What this means, in Hobbes's case, is that every reality is wholly

---

[1] Thomas Hobbes, *Leviathan, or the Matter, Forme and Power of a Commonwealth Ecclesiastical and Civil,* ed. with an introduction by Michael Oakeshott (Oxford: Basil Blackwell, n.d.), pp. 81–82.

[2] *Ibid.*, p. 64.

definable in terms of space, time, and laws of causation. The universe is composed of objects in motion; every reality has a definite location in space and time and is governed by invariable physical laws. A human being is simply one of the objects making up the universe; he is more complex than such things as rocks and trees, but not essentially different. What concerns us at this point is only one consequence of this view, that unity among human beings, as we usually understand it, is impossible. Material objects are essentially external to one another; they cannot be united by bonds such as compassion, empathy, or a common purpose. They can be united only in the sense of being put in the same place or forcibly joined together, as with stones in the building of a wall. For Hobbes men were material objects and he logically concluded that they could be united only by the power of an absolute government.

Many thinkers have argued that human beings are essentially united. Probably the most influential of these was Aristotle (384–322 B.C.), who expressed the ancient Greek feeling for the primary and all-pervasive reality of the city-state. For Aristotle, just as a leaf in its innermost nature is part of a tree, so man is thoroughly and inevitably a member of a city. "The man who is isolated — who is unable to share in the benefits of political association, or has no need to share because he is already self-sufficient — is no part of the polis [the city-state], and must therefore be either a beast or a god." [3]

Aristotle did not carry the concept of unity to its logical extreme, which would be the ideal of a global and completely egalitarian polity. Men could not unite on any wider scale, Aristotle believed, than that of the city-state; moreover, even within the city-state only a few could attain the full unity of common citizenship, most people being fitted only to be artisans, laborers, or even slaves. Despite these qualifications, however, Aristotle's political thought is a sober and powerful denial that human beings are essentially estranged. Perhaps his most famous utterance is that "man is a political being" —

[3] Aristotle, *Politics,* translated by Ernest Barker (Oxford: Clarendon Press, 1946), p. 6.

a being who cannot realize his essence in solitude and privacy but only in the company of fellow citizens.

But if it is true, as Aristotle argued, that human beings are not estranged by their very nature, how does it happen that throughout history peace and harmony have been so impermanent and elusive?

2

**If human beings are not estranged in essence,
why are there so many divisions and conflicts among them?**

This question presents a simple (although not easily resolved) issue: If human beings are not estranged in essence, the divisions and conflicts among them must proceed either from man himself or from circumstances external to man. Let us consider first the former alternative — that men cause estrangement even though they are not in essence estranged.

What could this mean? The answer is delineated as sharply as anywhere in the writings of Saint Augustine (354–430). Augustine held that God did not intend man to live in a state of division and conflict and hence these conditions were not attributable to the human essence, which had been created by God. What happened was that man had betrayed his essence. This betrayal was what Augustine and many other Christians meant by "sin." Man has carried out a tragic rebellion against the order of God's creation. In doing this he has rejected his nature as received from God and has become in actuality something other than what he was in essence. The unity of divine creation has been lost. Neither God nor the human essence created by God can be blamed for this dreadful derangement, but only man in his perversity.

To understand sin as Augustine envisioned it, however, it is crucial to realize that sin is not merely a *tendency* of the will; it is a settled and — humanly — unchangeable configuration of the will. Man not only commits particular wrongs; he does so out of a confirmed disorientation of soul. But he is still responsible not only for the particular wrongs he commits but also for the state of will from which they arise. It is this primal responsibility that is symbolized by the concept of original sin. Man finds himself an alien within creation, divided from both Creator and fellow creatures. So far as human powers go, this condition is irreparable; it is, at the same time, man's own fault. There is hope only in the grace of God.

Many people today are repelled by this kind of dark and censorious theology. It must be recognized, nevertheless, that Augustine's view is not just arbitrary dogma; it conforms with a strange but common experience. Many men feel unable to resist doing things for which they nevertheless condemn themselves; they thus feel helplessly estranged (assuming that the acts for which they condemn themselves are in some way antithetical to others), and at the same time guilty of producing their estrangement.

Augustine's is a fearful and impressive philosophy, with its picture of men as a ruined race toiling in a world where there is no light aside from the gleams of God's mercy. Equally powerful philosophies, however, have been founded on the idea of human innocence. This idea is old because, besides possibly being true, it is pleasant. Augustine devoted much time and effort to attacking Pelagius, a monk who argued that man has it within his own power to turn away from sin. But perhaps the most eloquent claims for human innocence are found in modern times, in the writings of Jean Jacques Rousseau (1712–1778).

If human beings are essentially united, and have never betrayed their essence, how has their history come to be filled with so much hatred and turmoil? The only possible answer is that they have in some way accidentally (and not because of grave, inherent defects in their nature) become entangled in circumstances that have estranged them from one another. It was Rousseau's conviction that a misfortune of this kind had occurred in the distant past. Early in man's career on earth, property and power came to be concentrated in the hands of a few. This did not happen because men were extremely evil, but it subverted the natural decency of men and the natural harmony of human relations. Rousseau's confidence in man did not lead him to palliate the evils of human society; on the contrary, he was one of the most bitter and radical social

critics of modern times. But he did not blame the disloca-
tions of society on man — at least, not on his essence and
not on any deliberate and irreversible repudiation of his
essence.

Augustinian and Rousseauean views of estrangement have
had powerful reverberations in other spheres of political
thought. For example, conceptions of the value and function
of established institutions are determined largely by the alternative that is chosen. According to the Augustinian philosophy, man is a dangerous being; existing social and political
institutions may be imperfect, but insofar as they assure some
kind of order, even if only through the pressures of habit and
fear, they have some value. From a point of view like Rousseau's, however, mere order is worth very little, for man is
capable of far greater things; he can attain justice and happiness. Rousseau saw the institutions of his time as keeping men
from being not Augustinian malefactors but Aristotelian fellow
citizens. This is not to say that Augustine always and Rousseau
never approved of established institutions. For Augustine, institutions are made by sinful men and are bound to have much
evil in them; Rousseau thought that the original virtue in man's
will had occasionally, as in the ancient Roman republic, es-
caped corruption and gained sovereign power. But for Augustine, heaven on earth is impossible and any order of life
precluding the hell implicit in man's nature deserves apprecia-
tion. For Rousseau, on the other hand, because man's innocence is not irretrievably lost, there is hope of earthly paradise,
and by this standard few actual societies can be seen as anything but mean and degraded.

Another way of stating the issue between Augustine and
Rousseau is this: Which is the primary source of evil, human
nature or institutions? For Augustine, the evil in institutions is
a result of the evil in human nature; Rousseau maintains the
opposite, that the evil in human nature is a consequence of the
evil in institutions. Thus for an Augustinian, the idea of man's
escaping the influence of institutions and recreating civilization
is unthinkable, whereas for a follower of Rousseau, such a
possibility is real.

This polarity suggests another aspect of the issue. A follower of Augustine, viewing man as evil and dangerous, can hardly help being nervous when human beings embark on radical political action. He is almost bound to be conservative — not in the sense of revering the prevailing order but in the sense of fearing any effort to change it. But a follower of Rousseau may well be revolutionary. Man's original innocence offers a potentiality for historical reconstruction. For this potentiality to be realized, of course, man in his primal decency must somehow throw off the influence of the oppressive and corrupting institutions in which he is encased. But nothing in Rousseau's thought forbids the hypothesis that this liberation is possible; the way is open even for surmising that in some circumstances the initial stages of revolutionary destruction might constitute the liberating act. As it happens, Rousseau himself was not so carefree about revolution, and he did not in fact assume that any act of institutional destruction was an act of liberation. The explosive effect of his thought in history, however, derived primarily from the revolutionary implications of his psychology — implications that Rousseau drew out cautiously, but his posterity exuberantly.

Recently in America a number of students and blacks have adopted a revolutionary attitude or at least have come to employ a revolutionary rhetoric. There is certainly enough evil in the established order, such as poverty and racial injustice, to warrant such an attitude. But is there enough goodness in man to warrant it? If it should be that Augustine is nearer the truth than Rousseau, then this radicalism, often infused with intolerance and self-righteousness, might lead to greater evils than those it attacks.

We have now considered the origin of estrangement — whether it lies in man's essence, in a tragic rejection of his essence, or merely in accidental historical circumstances. This discussion puts us in a position to ask how estrangement can be overcome, or, if human beings are estranged in essence, how the divisions and conflicts among them can be moderated. It may help, in considering this question, to focus on a human faculty that again and again since the beginnings of political philosophy, has been seen as the primary source of unity and order, that is, reason.

3

Can estrangement be overcome through reason?

There is no doubt as to the consensus of the West in relation to this question. It is strongly affirmative. Granted, of the two major roots of Western culture, the Hebraic and the Greek, in the former there was relatively little respect for reason, man's overriding duty being to obey the commands of God. However, divine-human relations sometimes involved rational discourse, as in the Book of Job. And in ancient Greece, the most powerful and prevalent theme of political thought was probably the idea that men can overcome misunderstanding and conflict through reason. The Greek view won the day and even Christianity became markedly rationalistic in the Middle Ages. Modern man thus inherited a strongly rationalistic tradition, which he has carried on most spectacularly in science and technology. While there have been some powerful revolts against the reigning rationalism, it would be difficult to say as yet that they have triumphed. Western man might still take as his motto the biblical injunction, "Come, let us reason together."

This consensus rests, however, on the assumption that human beings in essence are united or at least that their interests at some point coincide. If they were envisioned as essentially estranged and their interests altogether in conflict, then, of course, there would be little that reason could do. Far from drawing men together, reason would enable the most cunning and ruthless of them to gain the advantage over others. No great political thinker (not even Machiavelli) has argued in favor of using reason in this fashion. But according to Plato, at least two intellectual figures who were well known in his own time, Thrasymachus and Callicles, did so. For these two men, as Plato depicts them, reason was a dissolvent of the customs and baseless moral beliefs that sometimes lured superior men into subordinating their own interests to the interests of others.

If there is some point at which individual interests happen to coincide, however, even if human beings are essentially estranged and care nothing about one another except as means to individual satisfaction, then reason might draw men together by disclosing the underlying unity of their interests. Such an idea enters into one of the most enduring concepts in Western political thought, that government is based on a "social contract." This concept is illustrated by the views of Hobbes. As already shown, Hobbes regarded men as estranged in essence. Yet he did believe that all men have an interest in peace and thus in effective government. Reason, he thought, could make this congruence of individual interests indisputably clear and thus could save men from the "war of all against all" into which they otherwise would plunge owing to their essential estrangement. For Hobbes, each person is concerned only for his own safety; but reason shows him that for him to be safe he must enter into a contract to obey a government that secures the safety of all.

The Western faith in reason reaches its height with denial of essential estrangement. The idea that through reason we can discern our common essence and from this source derive the laws that unite us is among the oldest and most durable principles of our heritage. It was the first principle of Plato's elitist, city-state political philosophy; in Stoicism it became the basis of an egalitarian and universalist outlook; in the Middle Ages it retained its authority, although combined with the principles of orthodox Christianity; and in modern times it has been the theoretical foundation both of international law (limiting state power in its external application) and of constitutional government (limiting state power in its internal application). By using our reason, according to this view, we become members of a community that is not destroyed by the conflicts among nations and among classes. Our common membership in this universal society of reason enables us to place above power, with its ceaseless tendency to become brutal and limitless, standards that are rationally certain and morally unchallengeable. If there is any single indispensable idea in our past it is this one.

Nevertheless, several thinkers have viewed the idea either with reservations or with definite hostility. An indication of the power of the rationalist idea is that probably no great thinker has repudiated it altogether. But one who came near to doing so, and thus serves as a convenient example of the antirationalist position, is Edmund Burke (1729–1797). Burke candidly defended prejudice in place of reason. His writings show a belief in the essential unity of men that is as emphatic and unqualified as Aristotle's. But Burke did not trust reason to disclose the human essence with accuracy. He thought that established customs and traditions reflected the nature of man far more correctly than did the abstract conclusions of reason; and these customs and traditions, when enthroned in the human mind, are "prejudice."

Not only is man too deep and complex to be adequately guided by reason, according to Burke; he is too dangerous as well. Burke had an Augustinian view of man. Order needs the support of habit and of emotion, and thus it depends on institutions and traditions that are old, hallowed, and unquestioned. Prejudice thus is not only wiser than reason, but is also more powerful.

For Burke, then, estrangement is overcome only through an old and awesome set of institutions. The claim to understand man by reason manifests groundless pride; the result of this claim is to imperil the mutual understanding and respect that can be found in humble submission to the traditions, customs, and institutions inherited from the past.

The aim of this book is to define some of the main pathways of political thought but not every possible pathway. I do not mean to suggest that there are only a few alternative routes that a reflective person logically can follow. Thought is (and should be) ingenious in finding untraveled ways. Nevertheless, the terrain of thought does impose certain common tendencies on those who start from the same basic principles. Accordingly, what has to be noted here is that the division between the rationalist and the Burkean positions tends to define two basically different ways of looking at the social and political world. The following polarities, in their typical forms, derive from this distinction.

1. *Moral absolutism* versus *moral relativism*. Moral absolutism is the theory that there are moral standards independent both of the interests of individuals and societies and also of the

standards that happen to prevail in any particular time and place. The main form of moral absolutism in Western history is the idea of natural law, according to which there is a universal and eternal law based on the essence of man and discernible by reason. Plainly this idea expresses the conviction that reason does draw men together. Relativism has various forms (depending on what is held to determine morality and thus what morality is held to be relative to), but one of its main forms is the principle that good and evil are defined by each society. Burke was not an extreme relativist, for he believed that certain standards are incumbent on men regardless of the rules prevailing in their societies. But his regard for custom and tradition led naturally to an acceptance of many of the moral variations among times and places.

2. *Uniformity* versus *organic unity*. Reason can discover only the general — that which is common to many particulars; consequently, rationalism readily gives rise to a conception of unity in which there is emphasis on uniformity. In contrast, thinkers like Burke are likely to be particularly open not only to the differences that are sanctioned by moral relativism but also to those differences among individuals — for example, in character, talent, and vocation — that are coordinated in the organic unity of the group. A clear expression of this polarity can be seen in Aristotle's protest that Plato erased essential differences among persons in order to unite them. "It is," Aristotle complains, "as if you were to turn harmony into mere unison, or to reduce a theme to a single beat." [4]

3. *Radicalism* versus *conservatism*. To believe that we can comprehend man rationally may lead to the notion that we have the capacity and the right to destroy all of those ancient institutions that are resting on mere prejudice and to rebuild them in accordance with rational designs. Rationalism in this way gives rise to radicalism. Such pride, before the majestic and enigmatic past, infuriated Burke. He set against it the conservatism that necessarily follows from the principle that man's essence is disclosed only through custom and tradition. The kind of order that is built by generations of prudent

[4] *Ibid.*, p. 51.

statesmen cannot be deliberately constructed according to the counsels of reason, as Burke saw it. If one is fortunate enough to live within such an order, all he can do — and this is his overriding duty — is to respect and to guard it.

Can mere human faculties, however, overcome estrangement, even assuming that human beings are not essentially estranged? Asking this brings us to an issue that people today generally ignore. The spiritual atmosphere of our time seems to be one of religious doubt along with human self-confidence. Thus it is widely assumed that we neither need to, nor can, call on anything beyond the faculties of man for resolving our tensions and discords. But is this assumption so clearly true that it cannot be plausibly questioned? In the past, one of the most persistent and widespread convictions has been that a stable and decent society must rest on some kind of religious ground. Numberless generations, in all parts of the globe, have assumed that men can be properly related to one another only if they are properly related to the divine.

It would seem that in all humility we must seriously ask whether this is so.

4

Are we dependent in any way on the divine for overcoming estrangement?

Three general positions in relation to this question can be conveniently distinguished. The first is the self-confident humanism of modern man, which often is accompanied by atheism or agnosticism and by suspicion of organized religion. No historical lessons have sunk more deeply into the American mind, it seems, than those drawn from the religious wars in Europe and the Puritan theocracy in Massachusetts. Religious faith can be both divisive and despotic. This conviction has been reinforced for many by the secularism of Marx and other radicals. For Marx, religion was "the opium of the people," and socialists have traditionally dismissed it as "pie in the sky." The serious allegation behind such rhetoric is that religion makes men indifferent to the worldly sufferings of others and in this way is an enemy of community.

The ascendant ideal today accords with this humanism. Almost all responsible people at present assume that the time has finally come, after long ages during which the majority of human beings lived in squalor and ignorance, to meet the pressing needs of everyone. Our powers of organization and production make the continuance of physical want intolerable; we must now care for one another in a measure that corresponds with our powers. Most of those sharing this ideal, however, make the crucial assumption that its realization need not be hindered and may even be helped by the weakening of religious faith that has occurred during the past few centuries. After all, when men felt closely united with the divine, they were usually very imperfectly united with one another; often they were horrifyingly cruel to one another. Now perhaps the love and devotion once bestowed on God can be bestowed on our fellow men.

The humanist vision of unity can be a moving one. In its light we see ourselves as inhabiting a vast, indifferent universe, clinging together in our cosmic loneliness and interdependence. Even most of those who still believe in God seem to feel that such a vision will suffice, as religious faith declines, to undergird our common life and action.

In view of this humanist consensus, it is striking that the political thinkers of antiquity and the Middle Ages for the most part believed that unity of man with man depends on unity of man with the divine. The first great political philosophy set forth in the West, that of Plato (427–347 B.C.), exemplifies this viewpoint. If the injunction implicit in most twentieth-century social commentary is, "Forget the transcendent, and concentrate on one another," the injunction implicit in *The Republic* is, "Know first the transcendent, then consider one another."

Plato believed that beyond all the things we can see, hear, and touch there is a source from which these things draw their reality and value. He called this simply "the Good." He likened the Good to the sun, which makes it possible for living things to grow and be seen, thus suggesting that the Good makes it possible for all things to be and to be known. Like all of the rest of reality, humanity is looked upon from this point of view. The being and worth of man are reflections of the Good, and man and his needs can be understood only in the light shed by the Good. Accordingly, a major theme of *The Republic* is that organizing the best human life is possible only through supreme knowledge, under the sun of all being. Thus human affairs are centered on the transcendent. Those who are separated from this ultimate principle of life and value and truth cannot possibly attain any authentic unity. For Plato, the twentieth-century notion that we should ignore ultimate realities to concentrate on building a good society would have seemed as absurd as it would seem to us in the twentieth century were someone to suggest that we disregard the laws of astronomy and aerodynamics in order to expedite the exploration of space.

Not long after the time of Plato, Stoic philosophers began to develop a far more ecumenical and egalitarian concept of unity than Plato's; more will be said about this concept further along. The point that needs to be made here is that the new concept of unity still rested on religious foundations. For the Stoics, the entire universe was divine. The duties that bind human beings to one another are imposed by the divine order they inhabit. In this sense there is unity among human beings only through the omnipresence of the divine.

The Platonic-Stoic conception of the dependence of the social on the religious is the second general position relating to the question we are discussing (the first having been the humanistic outlook). What distinguishes it from the third position, to which we now turn, is its reliance on human initiative. The divine is conceived to be inert, and merely available; it is man who acts. For adherents of the third position, which is that of orthodox Christianity, it is God who acts.

The two positions are, in spite of this difference, at one in grounding authentic unity among human beings on unity with the divine. Thus in the Christian view a person is a worthy object of love owing to a sanctity that comes from God. For Paul, we (or at least all Christians) are "members one of another;" but this is only because we have been created and redeemed by God. It would have been as unthinkable to Paul as to Plato that human beings should love one another, or even respect one another, simply for what they are in themselves rather than for the divine splendor they reflect. The only authentic unity is, to borrow Augustine's phrase, that of "the City of God."

But the orthodox Christian idea of the relation of the divine and the human departs very far from that held by Plato and the Stoics. For the Greek thinkers man can ascend to God; this is a power inherent in reason. For Christians, however, the idea of man's ascending to God was an expression of pride. It was foolishly and sinfully unrealistic. The distance between man and God is far too vast for man to be able to cross it. Through sin man has removed himself from God's presence and has crippled himself as a spiritual being; thus unity with the divine is dependent on divine initiative. This initiative, for Christians, was taken through the life, death, and resurrection of Jesus.

What has happened, in sum, is that the idea of the ascent of man has been replaced by that of the descent of God.

As a result, the conquest of human discord came to be viewed very differently from the way it had been in the philosophy of the Greeks. For Plato and the Stoics it was sufficient that the divine was real; man could find his way to the high plateaus of divine reality and build his cities there. Even for those Greeks who emphasized the dependence of harmony on the divine, all cities were cities of man. Christians, however, necessarily saw things otherwise. No real community could be originated by man. Only God could break the chains cast by original sin and enable human beings to unite. The unity of man with man, no less than that of man with God, was seen as dependent on God's merciful descent into the morass of disorder and alienation that man had created. Community originates in the action, not merely the availability, of the divine. This is why any true city is a "City of God."

Today many people find it hard to take ideas of this kind very seriously. But for many centuries in the past they were taken very seriously indeed, and one would have to be deeply complacent to assume that it is altogether the advanced state of our own intellects that makes the profoundest concerns of earlier ages so incomprehensible to us.

At the very least, we should bring ourselves to ask what we mean when we speak of "the dignity of the individual." This is perhaps the key phrase for expressing the modern ideal of community; each human being, according to this ideal, deserves respect and hence fair treatment, whatever his race or faith or class. Few people would be disposed to attack this standard; perhaps because it calls forth a sense of the ultimate or perhaps mainly because of cultural conditioning, it has immense authority. On the basis of a humanistic outlook, however, does it really make any sense? Plato believed that the Good, the sun of all being, might become incarnate in a few human beings — in philosophers; he thought that all human beings had at least some capacity for reflecting this supreme source of light and reality. Jews and Christians believe that "God created man in his own image." [5] According to the Christian faith God is so concerned for the redemption of each individual that he sacrificed his own Son to this end. One may find such patterns of belief incomprehensible or implausible, but they did provide a context in which it makes sense to speak of "the dignity of the individual."

If the divine is nowhere in the picture, however, what qualities entitle every individual to the deep respect that is called for when we use the word "dignity?" If there is no Platonic sun of being, no God, can there still be glory in every man? People today readily say that there can. Is it apparent, then, to the dispassionate eye of observation and reason? This is doubtful. Dignity is not a plain empirical fact that we can perceive in human beings as we can perceive the color of their hair and the shapes of their noses. But if the dignity of every individual is not a plain empirical fact and cannot be derived from any principle concerning the transcendent, then is it anything at all? Is it real?

It would be well for us, in the twentieth century, if we were able to answer this question, for the individual seems to be threatened from all sides. "The organization man," "the lonely crowd," "the revolt of the masses," and like phrases are well-known signals of alarm in which writers have expressed the pervasive sense that the individual is being engulfed and lost. But how can we save him if we really do not know what we mean when we speak of "the dignity of the individual?"

[5] Genesis 1:27.

The question is posed perhaps more dramatically than anywhere else in the writings of Fyodor Dostoevsky (1821–1881).
For Dostoevsky the issue lay between two radically antagonis-
tic ideals, that of the "man-god" and that of the "God-man."
The former is the ideal of one who has repudiated God and has
embarked on the enterprise of elevating man to the status of
God. Dostoevsky believed such an enterprise to be a logical
and inevitable outgrowth of atheism. Its results, however, he
saw as being far from the global compassion that is invoked by
humanitarian atheists and agnostics in the twentieth century.
He thought that the denial of God was in effect also a denial of
the dignity of individuals and of the authority of all moral
laws. Thus the man-god would become a criminal, a nihilistic
revolutionary, or a tyrant.

Not only did Dostoevsky reject the atheism and agnosticism
that are so common at present; he rejected also the widespread
sentiment — shared even by believers — that whether one is
an atheist or an agnostic is purely a private matter. On the
contrary, these attitudes imperil even the minimal decencies in
society at large. Dostoevsky would say that the God-denying
but humanitarian people who are so numerous today simply
have not yet realized the real meaning of their own faithless-
ness.

The God-man, in Dostoevsky's mind, was an entirely different matter. Christ is the original God-man. The ideal of the
God-man is that of mankind exalted to divine status through
the mercy of God rather than through the assertiveness of
men. The ideal can be realized only through Christianity.
Hence the decline of Christianity, which has become more
pronounced in the twentieth century than it was in Dostoevsky's time, but which Dostoevsky prophetically foresaw, was in
his eyes an all-engulfing catastrophe.

The four questions so far discussed have enabled us to consider human relations in their most general character. We
have asked about both the source and the healing of estrangement. More exactly, we have asked whether human beings are
estranged in essence, and if not how the human essence has
been lost and can be restored.

It would be possible at this point to conclude the chapter
and to move into other areas of thought. Some of the ideas

discussed may become more alive, however, if we reflect on their application to the most serious divisions among men. Over the centuries, the two most profound and unbridgeable divisions seem to have been those among peoples (city-states, empires, and nations) and those among classes. These will be the subjects of the final two questions of this chapter.

5

Should all peoples be united in a single global society?

The history of thought discloses two extreme and opposed responses to this question. Both are old and enduring; both appear in ancient and in modern times as well.

Greeks in the age of Socrates and Plato believed that a political order even as large as the modern nation-state was incompatible with a fully human life. Aristotle's assertion that "man is a political being" expressed a widely shared conviction; it was commonly assumed, however, that man can live according to his political nature only where states are small. To live in a large state or in an empire is to be governed from a distant center and thus to be a subject rather than a citizen. In Aristotle's vision, men are united by a universal essence, yet only a parochial state, the *polis,* can enable them to realize that essence and the unity it implies.

This is plainly a vision in which the idea of a single, global society is threatening and antihuman.

It is a vision which, in modern times, has recurred with increasing frequency as people have sought ways of escaping the impersonality and inhuman scale of industrial civilization. Thus Rousseau reaffirmed the basic standard of ancient democracy — that a state should be small enough for the citizens to meet regularly in a single assembly. Since the time of Rousseau, some of the most idealistic thinkers have felt that only through breaking up the vast states and organizations of the modern world could community be saved. And in contemporary America most radicals seem to believe that the only way to a new humanity is through drastic decentralization. Indeed, the ideas of community and of face-to-face association have become practically equivalent in many minds. From this point of view, for all mankind to fall under a single government and to constitute a single society, would be catastrophic.

Another kind of idealism, however, is inspired by a very different vision. It is a vision of all human beings, with no peoples or races excluded, organizing and living their common humanity in a global commonwealth. This conception, like its opposite, that of face-to-face democracy, arose in ancient times. It was developed by the Stoics after the city-states had been incorporated in empires. The *polis* is replaced, in the thought of the Stoics, by the *cosmopolis* — the cosmic *polis*. As we know, the universe is a divine order in Stoic thought; this order is present in laws that can be apprehended by reason; we are all therefore citizens of a universal city. Here the principle that there is a universal human essence takes what seems a very logical political form: the ideal of a universal human community. It is not surprising that Stoicism was the principal philosophy embraced by the most effective statesmen of universal order that the world has ever known — those who administered the Roman Empire and shaped the Roman law.

Christian thinkers during antiquity and the Middle Ages were if anything more universalist than the Stoics, for typically they envisioned mankind as united not only by natural law but also by the divine plan of redemption, and these two forms of unity, they thought, should be recognized and acted upon both through some kind of universal political order and through the Catholic (which is to say world-embracing) Church.

The Roman ideal of universal and eternal peace and the Christian ideal of one global faith linger as a bitter longing in the twentieth century. These ideals glimmer faintly in our international law and in the United Nations. Their presence is most evident, perhaps, in the kind of horror we feel before the maelstrom of nationalism, fanaticism, and war in which we seem about to be submerged.

One of the most powerful restatements of the universalist outlook is found in the philosophy of Marx. Nations are held by Marxists to be organizations of a doomed class; the workers will establish the lasting and all-encompassing unity that finally eluded both the Roman Empire and the Roman Church. But how far we are from realizing this ancient dream is indicated by the contributions of Marxism itself to the self-righteousness and belligerence of some nations and to the ideologies setting us against one another.

Which do we really want, associations so small and personal that they might, as Aristotle believed, be bound together by friendship, or a peace so inclusive and just that in its compass all mankind is one fraternity? Is our ideal Athens or Rome? These two visions have been invested with such splendor by their idealistic defenders that one may feel let down when reminded that many prefer what we now have, the nation-state system that crystallized about five hundred years ago. This is another alternative to the single, global society which we are considering.

Is the nation-state just the wrong size — too large for personal relations and too small for global concord? Most people prior to the Reformation would have said that it is, and many today would agree. The nation-state is vast and impersonal; individuals and their intimate, spontaneous relations seem to be nothing before the nation and its demands for money, for soldiers, for trained technicians, and for submissive and law-abiding workers. The hatred that many students feel for "the Establishment," the draft, the Pentagon, and so forth, probably arises in some part from their sense of the vulnerability of personal relations before the overwhelming and omnipresent power of the nation. At the same time, however, no single nation can guarantee global peace, and thus its might is dedicated above all to war; it brings the impersonality of the global state but not the security and peace. Professors and students both seem to have felt these defects keenly. In universities today the nation-state has few friends.

During the past two centuries, however, it has been one of the chief objects of human devotion. And not only on the part of the worst human beings; men of intelligence and high ideals have been nationalists. An example is the great German philosopher Georg W. F. Hegel (1770–1831).

Hegel believed that for a community to have any real life it must have some significance in history; it must play a part in the affairs of mankind. Occasionally in the past, it is true, small associations have been able to do this; Athens is the outstanding example. Hegel apparently believed, however, that life now had to be conducted on a larger scale. The nation-state could attain a degree of power and of inner diversification beyond the reach of smaller associations. At the same time, however, a community should not be coextensive with that vast and miscellaneous collection of people that we call "mankind." It would then have no identity as a particular community. To have this identity, it must be distinct from other communities — in a position to define itself through its differences from them, and to test itself against them in war. On these grounds, Hegel looked on Athens and Rome — the small and the universal — both as stages that have been left behind in the progressive development of humanity. The climax of history, he thought, will occur in the era of nation-states.

These political bodies took on a religious grandeur in Hegel's thought. A nation is of greater reality and value, he held, than any individual human being. And in one of the most notorious propositions contained in the literature of political thought he referred to the nation-state as "the Divine Idea as it exists on earth." [6] Hegel has been condemned and derided for such statements. He only said explicitly and philosophically, however, what many modern nationalists have felt.

Hegel was more extreme, however, than one has to be in order to defend the nation-state and in that way to answer the present question negatively. It is possible to feel on the one hand that polities no larger than the ancient city-states are in most circumstances too small to be economically viable, militarily defensible, or culturally profound and diversified. It is possible to feel at the same time, however, that it would be presumptuous and oppressive to place the entire globe under one set of institutions. These polar attitudes are apt to leave one favoring something like the present nation-state — a political order that is large but less than global.

[6] Georg Wilhelm Friedrich Hegel, *The Philosophy of History*, rev. ed. (New York: Wiley, 1900), p. 39.

From this point of view the nation, with all of its flaws, may seem an indispensable medium for uniting the individual with others. Only as a member of a nation does one enter into the full range of human relationships — those involved in family, vocation, military responsibilities, and so forth. One can hold this view, be it noted, while admitting that one's nation is very imperfect and that one's fellow citizens (and presumably oneself with them) have much to be forgiven. There is, in short, a sober and repentant nationalism that rejects not only the ideal of a single, global society but also national self-glorification of the kind underwritten by Hegel.

Who is more nearly right — the Athenian citizen, the Roman-Christian universalist, or the modern nationalist? Each one feels that he speaks for an indispensable condition of unity and life.

Let us now, by means of a final question, reflect on unity among classes.

6

Should all class distinctions be abolished?

Let us assume that unity is good and that our end is to overcome estrangement. In that case this question presents us with two subordinate questions. The first is whether class distinctions necessarily are in the way of unity. It is possible to argue, after all, that unity depends on the coordination of differences; if that is so, a properly arranged set of class distinctions might be a prerequisite rather than an obstacle to unity.

The second subordinate question we confront is whether it is possible to abolish all class distinctions. There is a dilemma here. If no unity can be achieved without abolishing classes, and if unity is good, it follows not only that classes should be abolished but also that this could only be done through violence, for classes that are in no way united would be unable to agree peacefully to their own abolition. But does not the use of violence, when as systematic and prolonged as in this case it presumably would have to be, itself promote class distinctions by advancing those who command the violence into a separate and dominant class? This dilemma, perhaps, is the contradiction — as fatal as any that Marx saw in capitalism — that has wrecked the hopes of the Russian Revolution.

As we consider the question of abolishing classes, then, let us keep in mind both the relationship that class distinctions bear to unity and the possibility that the very project of abolishing classes is self-defeating.

The affirmative answer that was contained in the research and thought of Karl Marx (1818–1883) shook Western institutions more profoundly than has any other utterance since the Reformation. The key to Marx's attitude lay in the importance he attributed to economic conditions. Marx held that man's ideas and feelings — in truth his whole nature — are shaped by his economic situation. This is to speak very generally. Marx was aware both that situations are usually complex, bringing a variety of pressures to bear on those experiencing them, and that individuals differ in the ways they appraise and respond to situations. On the whole, however, Marx believed that how people think and feel will be determined by how they work. One must work in order to live; but in order to work one must accept a place in the economic system, and the nature of that place will determine his entire situation in life. It is manifest from history and from anthropological and sociological studies that human nature is not fixed but is malleable. We may infer that the character of human beings will be shaped by the life situations inherent in their work.

This view may seem at first glance to be innocuous and sensible. It implies, however, that the classes must be composed of completely different kinds of people and that they cannot possibly be united in a single community. Marx defined classes in economic terms because his emphasis on the formative power of economic circumstances allowed no other differentia to be of primary significance. He saw the main class division as being between people who own nothing and thus have to work and people who own property and thus command the resources on which the lives of all others depend. Between these two groups there is not simply a divergence of interests or ways of life. One is almost tempted to say there is a divergence of species, for their completely different economic situations make them completely different beings.

Reverting to the concepts we have been discussing in this

chapter, this differentiation amounts to a denial (1) that there is a common human essence uniting men and (2) that there are common, impartial faculties, such as reason, by which any such essence can be discerned.

As for (1), according to Marx a human being cannot be identified with any abstract, changeless idea of man. Rather, he *is* what he *does;* hence his nature is defined by his work. Those who do different kinds of work, therefore, such as wage laborers and capitalists, must be very different in nature and have little or nothing in common. As for (2), even so far as there is some very general human essence by virtue of which both laborers and capitalists are human, there are no common, impartial faculties powerful enough to define this essence accurately and to bring everyone to respect it. Man's ideas and feelings about life in general are products of his economic situation and so must be his ideas and feelings about his own essence. Thus not only are owners and workers very different in nature, they have different conceptions of themselves.

It is apparent that for Marx there could be no unity among the classes even if there were no serious conflict of interest dividing them. As a matter of fact, however, Marx believed that there was such a conflict. Owners of the means of production (these are primarily factories in the era of industrialism, but earlier they consisted in land) are compelled by the productive system to oppress the workers. In other words, all productive systems, aside from communism, are essentially exploitative. It follows that the exploited cannot remain satisfied with moderate reforms; they are driven to attack the entire economic order within which they live and work. The owners are of course the custodians and beneficiaries of the established order. Thus the two classes are not only different; they are antagonists in a deadly war.

It follows that any social order claiming to unite all classes is basically fraudulent. Ruling classes always claim that the populace is at one in accepting their governance and the ideology behind it; but this is no better than an effort to disguise the despotism they impose. The liberal democracies, in Marx's eyes, were covert dictatorships on the part of capitalists. In an opinion to which a number of present-day students and blacks subscribe, Marx held that modern democracy is only a façade; it cannot be, as it purports to be, the rule of the people, inasmuch as the interests of those being ruled are in fundamental and incurable opposition to the interests of their rulers.

Thus Marx provided one answer to the question of whether class divisions are an obstacle to unity. What about the question of abolishing these distinctions? How can this be done without using violence in a way that gives rise to new distinctions while suppressing the old ones?

Here Marx appealed to what he saw as the natural course of history. This course he believed was toward the abolition of private ownership and therefore toward a society without classes. Development in this direction did not depend primarily on deliberate human planning but would be the result of tensions inherent in the capitalist system. Thus a group using force to abolish classes, when the time is ripe, would only serve as a midwife for history and would not need to embark on the kind of sustained and systematic violence that might create a new class. And for Marx, of course, economic circumstances form human beings, not political circumstances; common ownership of the means of production would bar the rise of a new governing class.

Among the philosophies opposed to Marxism in the matter of class relations, two principal types can be distinguished: the conservative and the liberal.

In conservatism of the kind represented by Edmund Burke, class divisions are assumed to be just and necessary. Societies need ruling groups, and some men are particularly well fitted, both by innate ability and by educational and other advantages, which cannot in the nature of things be enjoyed by everyone, to be members of these ruling groups. Moreover, it is assumed not only that class distinctions are justified but that the lower classes can see that they are justified. Thus the conservative idea is that of unity *through* class distinctions, which conforms with the possibility noted at the outset of this discussion: Class distinctions are a prerequisite, rather than an obstacle, to unity. Class lines required by a sense of justice in which all classes share are not lines of estrangement but are rather articulations of the structure giving unity to the whole.

To put this in terms of the central concepts of this chapter:

Through loyalty to common traditions and customs, all classes participate in the "prejudice" that unites them. This prejudice discloses man's essence, on which unity is based. Here the human essence is realized not through the absolute uniformity and equality envisioned by some radicals, but by the simultaneous diversity and unity of classes.

In this view, no problem exists as to how classes can be abolished, for they should not be abolished but preserved. Conservatives point to the apparent impossibility of abolishing one class system without creating a new one as evidence that class distinctions are inevitable and that it is vain for man to oppose such necessities with will and violence.

The most effective opposition to Marxism has probably come from those who hold that while justice does not sanction the division of society into separate and unequal classes, all classes can perceive the requirements of justice and thus can cooperate in eradicating class distinctions. This is the central idea in iiberalism of the kind represented by Franklin D. Roosevelt and John F. Kennedy. Thus, in answering the question of whether class distinctions necessarily stand in the way of unity, most liberals would agree more nearly with Marx than with Burke. Granted, many liberals would be satisfied with moderating class distinctions rather than totally doing away with them. Nevertheless, liberalism is generally on the side of equality and is not easily reconciled with the Burkean idea that class differences contribute to social unity.

In answering the question of the possibility of abolishing class distinctions, liberals generally differ both from Marx and from Burke. They feel that class distinctions cannot be abolished (or moderated) by force but nevertheless they must be abolished (or greatly moderated). The means of doing this is the community of reason that transcends class divisions. The classes should unite, it is held, not in accepting society but in reforming it. All classes should come together in a single community, as called for by conservatism, but not in one that remains what it has always been; they should come together rather in a reforming community, a community that is imperfect but that can gradually perfect itself.

Two ideas we have discussed are at the core of the liberal

outlook: that men are essentially at one, and that reason enables them peacefully to realize their unity. A common essence and common rational faculties are in the final analysis of greater force than the economic system. Owners may not gladly give up unfair privileges, but they can be brought, by reason and legal pressure, peacefully to do so. Marx's basic premises — that man is made by his economic situation and that the classes are in mortal conflict — largely rule out the possibility of any such understanding between owners and workers. This is why Marx was a revolutionary rather than a reformer: Unity would normally have to be created through violent destruction of the owning class. Liberalism, in contrast, rests on the idea that economic estrangement is not total estrangement; a common human essence dictating harmony and common rational powers making this harmony accessible remain, despite all class divisions.

This faith has been of tremendous historical importance. It has been professed in one way or another by most of the governing parties in the Western democracies during the present century. It has provided the main ground on which the totalitarian extremes of Fascism and Communism have been opposed. But is it a valid faith?

For most of those who are not hungry and cold, liberalism is a more *appealing* faith than is Marxism. It does not tell us that we live in a doomed society or that we are obliged to take on the discomforts and perils of revolutionary action. It regards all men with affection and hope.

But is liberalism a *truer* faith than is Marxism? It requires some complacency to say without hesitation that it is. We see more and more clearly how skillfully, through several decades of social reform, beginning with the New Deal in 1933, the owning classes have preserved their wealth and their privileges. Further, we see now that under the governance of these classes cities have decayed, nature has been debauched, and the wealth of the nation has been squandered in a futile and barbarous war. It is no longer so easy to count on the possibilities of peaceful reform or to regard all men with a liberal affection and hope.

But most of us cannot stand on the Marxist side, either,

without serious misgivings. These are occasioned above all, perhaps, by the implications of the Marxist vision of the warfare of classes. If capitalists and workers are irreconcilable enemies, has mankind any prospect before it except despotism and terror? After all, Marx presented an extremely somber picture of man's situation. He did not succumb to despair because he shared the nineteenth-century faith in the common people and in historical progress. But today our faith in the common people has been shaken by such phenomena as the vulgarity of popular culture; our faith in historical progress has been ravaged by the catastrophic events of our time. In these circumstances, what remains of Marxism spells despair.

In concluding this chapter, it should be pointed out that all of the doubts to which this and the preceding question give rise are expressions of the simple issues set forth in connection with the first four questions. Let these be summarily restated. Are the hatred and violence of the twentieth century mirrors in which we see ourselves as we basically and inescapably are? If not, how is it that such misfortunes have come to pass, and how can we gain and enact a deeper vision? Through what faculties? And through what powers — those of man alone?

SUGGESTED READINGS

(Titles are listed chronologically. All are available in paperback or other inexpensive editions.)

Plato, *The Symposium*
———. *The Republic,* Books I–IV
Aristotle. *Politics,* Books I–III, VII–VIII
Saint Augustine. *The City of God,* Chapters 11–14
Dante Alighieri. *On World-Government (De Monarchia)*
Saint Thomas Aquinas. *The Political Ideas of St. Thomas Aquinas.* Ed. by Dino Bigongiari. (Hafner)
Hobbes, Thomas. *Leviathan,* First Part
Rousseau, Jean Jacques. *The Social Contract*
Burke, Edmund. *Reflections on the French Revolution*

Paine, Thomas. *The Rights of Man*

Marx, Karl. *Economic and Philosophical Manuscripts*

Marx, Karl and Engels, Friedrich. *Basic Writings on Politics and Philosophy.* Ed. by Lewis Feuer. (Doubleday)

Durkheim, Emile. *Suicide.*

Buber, Martin. *I and Thou*

Freud, Sigmund. *Civilization and Its Discontents*

Bergson, Henri. *The Two Sources of Morality and Religion*

Berdyaev, Nicolas. *Slavery and Freedom*

Fromm, Erich. *Escape from Freedom*

Niebuhr, Reinhold. *The Nature and Destiny of Man,* Vol. I

Dawson, Christopher. *Religion and Culture*

Marcuse, Herbert. *Eros and Civilization*

3

Inequality and Equality

Taking up the problem of inequality carries us into the center of modern political conflicts. The history of recent times could be told largely in terms of the rebellion against privilege and power that began with the French Revolution in 1789. Socialism and communism have both been deliberate, long-sustained assaults on inequality; the twentieth-century upheavals in Asia and Africa have been inspired by the determination that wealth and world power shall not be monopolized by white men; and in America much turmoil has been created by the student attack on "the Establishment" and by the black revolt against the ancient white ascendancy.

Taking up the problem of inequality also reminds each one of us of some of the major circumstances of his own life. In practically all times and places men have been divided by inequalities of rank, power, and wealth. They still are. Granted, some important changes have occurred in the last century or two. Traditional aristocracies have largely disappeared; the physical lives of the multitudes have become far more comfortable and probably on the whole more secure than in any earlier age; governments in many countries have come to depend for their power on the votes of the people; predominant styles and values in many societies have come to be those embraced by the common people. Even though we do not yet understand the full significance of these changes, it would be impossible to claim that they are without great meaning; they may be leading us into — or already have led us into — a new era of history. Nevertheless, marked inequalities of rank, power, and wealth remain in every nation, and the life of everyone is decisively affected with respect to material decency, education, associations, and vocation by the level on which it is lived.

Thus inequality and equality are not merely abstractions which can be safely and responsibly ignored, even if one prefers not to think about them. They form an issue that has so much to do with the history of our times and with the circumstances in which each one lives that we are compelled to give them thought.

The logical starting point for this undertaking is a question that parallels Question 1 in the preceding chapter. There it was asked whether it is in the fundamental nature of things or the result merely of historical circumstances that men are estranged. Here it must be asked whether, beneath all of the inequalities incorporated in the social and political order, men are really — by nature and not just by convention — unequal.

7

Are human beings unequal in essence?

Certainly human beings are unequal in most of their physical and psychological characteristics. They are unequal in health and intelligence and emotional balance and in so many other ways that it would be tedious to try to list them. It is easy to see, however, that these unassailable facts are far from deciding the issue.

To start with, one must ask whether such apparently *natural* inequalities are in reality merely the results of *social* inequalities. May not poor health, for example, derive from the inadequate nutrition that is apt to go along with poverty, and may not low intelligence merely reflect the illiteracy of an impoverished household? Clearly in some cases the answer is affirmative. It does not seem, however, that all inequalities can be traced back to social causes. The difficulty encountered in try-ing to do this is that marked inequalities are manifest among people who have been shaped by the same conditions. Among those who have been raised in the most propitious physical circumstances, some are healthier than others, and among those who have had the greatest educational advantages, some manifest greater intelligence than others. Hence there seems to be no escaping the fact of natural inequality.

Still, a shadow of doubt remains. No two people ever grow up within *exactly* the same circumstances, and differences that appear minor to an outside observer may be decisive for those molded by them.

Concerning another aspect of the matter, there is more than a shadow of doubt: Do the inequalities that we can measure pertain to the essence of the human being measured? For ex-ample, when we gauge the intelligence of someone, are we gauging the entire capacity of his consciousness or only his ability to carry on certain intellectual operations that happen to be emphasized in our culture? Certainly we are not in touch with another person's essence when we appraise him by stan-dards that have no absolute and universal validity. But one's doubts about judgments of inequality may go more deeply than this. Let us assume that an absolute standard of intelli-gence has been discovered so that when we measure intelli-gence we measure the entire capacity of consciousness. Does even a measurement of this kind pertain to the essence of the human being measured? Is intelligence or any other particular quality part of the essence of a human being?

The question may be put in this way: Is it possible that someone who is markedly and demonstrably inferior to most others in health, intelligence, emotional balance, and other good qualities is yet *in essence* equal to everyone else? The idea sounds strange. Yet we seem to say something of this kind when we say that there is an inherent dignity in every individ-ual or that each person should be treated as an end and not merely as a means.

Today it may seem that idealism is on the side of equality and that there is something cynical in the idea that human beings are essentially unequal; for to say that they are essentially unequal is to say that they are unequally human. Nevertheless, some of the most exalted figures in Western intellectual history have been willing to say this. Aristotle is a good example. He envisioned mankind as a great natural hierarchy, with the main determinant of rank being the degree and kind of reason one possesses. At the summit of the hierarchy are those preeminent in their powers of general understanding, such as scientists and philosophers. Beneath them in order come natural citizens, who are rational enough to manage political affairs in company with many others of their kind, and then natural artisans and workers, who should not take part in political affairs. At the base of the hierarchy are men with only enough reason to perform services for others; they are slaves by nature. Aristotle defined man in terms of reason; hence, to have only enough reason to be an artisan or worker is to be deficient in humanity, and to be a natural slave is to be hardly a human being at all. Aristotle would have regarded as a palpable and dangerous absurdity the later Christian notion that a person who is fitted neither for science and philosophy nor for political activity may nevertheless stand at the summit of a hidden hierarchy of grace.

Views of Aristotle's kind, maintaining the essential inequality of men, usually assume one of two main forms. For some, the superiority of the few consists in their relationship with a transcendent being — with "the Good" or with God; from this point of view men are unequal in sanctity. One of the greatest proponents of this outlook was Plato. In Plato's vision a few men were superior in essence to all others; these were philosophers who had ascended to a knowledge of the Good. Their supremacy consisted essentially in their relationship with the divine.

Let us note in passing that this view is more paradoxical and harder to understand than it may seem to be at first glance. The human essence, in terms of which superiority is defined, is not seen as contained within the individual as a separate and self-enclosed entity; it must be thought of rather as lying within the relationship of the individual and the Good. Strictly speaking, therefore, the philosopher's essential superiority to others does not consist in his superior intelligence but in the transcendental relationship to which his intelligence gives him access.

For certain other thinkers the excellence of the best men is purely worldly. It consists in such qualities as political genius, artistic mastery, and athletic prowess. Excellence does not depend on any sort of transcendental relationship but is entirely within the person. It might be said to consist, at least for some thinkers, not in being *related* to the divine but in *being* divine.

The writings of Friedrich Nietzsche (1844–1900) constitute an extreme and moving statement of this belief. Nietzsche was convinced that one condition determined the spiritual atmosphere and the duty of serious men in his time: an awakening to the unreality of God. His melodramatic proclamation of this condition is by now a familiar phrase in the ears of everyone: "God is dead." It has thus become incumbent on man to rise up out of the self-destructive humility imposed on him by Christianity and to affirm his full worldly being. What does this mean? What is the nature of man's worldly being? According to Nietzsche, it is "the will to power." Being is power, and it is in the nature of man ceaselessly to transcend himself and thus to search for greater and greater power. Hence if man is now to affirm himself, taking up the cosmic room which once, so to speak, was filled by God, he must unapologetically dedicate himself to the enhancement of his power. This did not necessarily mean political activity and war; a great artist, Nietzsche thought, might be more powerful than a Roman emperor. But it did mean inequality.

Nietzsche repeatedly, and with utmost bitterness, attacked the idea of equality, which he saw as one of the devices by which the masses, in their pettiness and rancor, crush human greatness. The average man is weak, and the grandeur of humanity thus depends on those with the daring and the strength to raise themselves far above the vast herds of common people. Now that "God is dead," human existence depends for its splendor and significance on the few who, rather than worshipping transcendent gods, become gods themselves. But this means that the idea of equality, cultivated for ages by Christians and pressed on the modern world by socialists and other reformers, must be thrust aside. Human relations must again, as in ancient times, be formed by domination and rank.

Plato and Nietzsche, both maintaining that human beings in essence are unequal, are among the greatest names in the history of the Western spirit. Despite such authority, however, one of the most irrepressible and potent ideas ever conceived is that all inequalities in the final analysis are insignificant and that human beings are essentially equal. This idea had much to do with the French Revolution, with the rise of socialism and communism, and with the twentieth-century revolutions in Russia and China; today it has helped to inspire the uprisings of black people in America and of the nonindustrial countries in Asia and Africa. What is the basis of such an idea?

Nietzsche was right in associating the idea of equality with faith in God. The first philosophical defense of the idea seems to have come from the later Stoics, with their belief in the divinity of the cosmos. Men were held to be equal in that each one could understand the main demands of the moral law implicit in the surrounding cosmic order. Thus they were equal in their relationship with the divine. If the idea of equality was planted in the Western mind by the Stoics, it deepened its roots and grew under the care of Christians. But here too, of course, equality was not measured by strength, or intelligence, or any other worldly characteristic. It was measured by God's creative and merciful omnipotence. Every man was formed by God and every man, having betrayed his origins, was offered redemption. Before the glory and hope surrounding God's descent into the world, all natural and social distinctions — health, intelligence, and beauty no less than rank, power, and wealth — faded into irrelevance.

Transcendentalism remained in the concept of equality that helped to inspire the rise of modern liberalism and democracy. John Locke (1632–1704), for example, who defended the establishment of constitutional (that is, lawful or limited) government in England and who influenced the framers of the American Constitution, clearly did not believe men to be equal in their observable qualities. They were, for Locke, equal only in the rights received from God. In like fashion Thomas Jefferson (1743–1826) asserted that men were *created* equal and that they were endowed *by their Creator* with inalienable rights.

Thus the idea of a sanctity that is received through a relationship with the divine is the basis not only of a certain conception of essential rank and inequality, as in Plato; it is the basis also of the traditional idea of essential equality.

Among the great political thinkers only one, Thomas Hobbes, maintained that in their purely worldly qualities men are essentially equal. However, his argument is not likely to appeal to those who desire, without believing in God, to believe in "the dignity of the individual," for in Hobbes's view men are less deserving of equal respect than of equal disdain. Our equality lies in our common subjection to human limitations and desires and, above all, in our common subjection to death. Hobbes sardonically pointed to the equalizing power of death with the observation that any man can kill any other (a point tragically illustrated in the assassination of President Kennedy, which was apparently produced by the determination of a profoundly alienated young man forcibly to rise above obscurity and insignificance). And not only are all of us mortal; all of us are governed by the egotistical desire to postpone death as long as we possibly can. This is where the interests of human beings coincide, despite their essential estrangement, making it possible to organize a society that is advantageous for everyone. Hobbes's egalitarian outlook did not rest wholly on death; he looked very skeptically on all of the supposed virtues and merits in which people take pride and was exceedingly deft in the art of puncturing pretensions. He conveyed the impression, however, that death was the sovereign equalizer. Thus, if all worldly rank and excellence, in the eyes of Christians, melted into insignificance before God in his mercy and omnipotence, in the eyes of Hobbes this happened in the face of inescapable death.

In sum, the foundation of traditional egalitarianism is religion. Where does this leave contemporary man, who is skeptical of God and the soul but is convinced of "the dignity of the individual?" Many people today assent to Nietzsche's declaration that the time has come for us to rely on our own intelligence and courage and not upon God. But most of them refuse to take seriously Nietzsche's insistence that when it comes to intelligence and courage and other qualities man presumably needs if he is to take the place of God, we are drastically unequal; instead they continue, with Christians, to exalt the common man. Does this make sense?

The question, in brief, is whether the idea of equality necessarily presupposes that of transcendence. Can we say that all men are equal without appealing to something beyond what we can see and measure?

This issue is involved in some of the most pressing concerns of our time. Despite centuries of equalization, inequality remains a stubborn and nagging reality. It is manifest in the acute poverty which persists even in a country as wealthy as the United States, in vast concentrations of private wealth, in the immense hierarchical organizations which dominate economic life in the industrial nations, and in the overwhelming power that has accumulated in the hands of modern governmental executives, with this exemplified most strikingly by the American presidency. The question is whether in the face of conditions such as these the cause of equality is doomed by the secularism of its defenders, that is, by their inability to appeal to any source of dignity beyond the plain, empirical character of the average man, with all of its manifest limitations and faults.

However one responds to this issue, the position he takes will have a large part in shaping his views of how society should be organized. Let us consider this aspect of the matter.

8

If some human beings are essentially superior to all others, how and by whom can they be identified?

First of all it must be asked whether the best men, if there are such men, can be identified at all. It is a powerful temptation to assume that they can, for it is humbling and exasperating to think that we might be arranged in some kind of unseen hierarchy, with manifest distinctions thus nullified and the worth of everyone placed in question. Plato, Aristotle, and Nietzsche all provide a measure of reassurance in this matter. Granted, most of us cannot determine the true rank of human beings (nor congratulate ourselves on our own worth and eminence). Nevertheless, the rank of human beings can be humanly known, and the order of society can be regulated so that it corresponds with that rank.

The whole idea that excellence lies in a certain relationship with the transcendent, however, rather than in observable, worldly qualities, forces anyone entertaining that idea to wonder whether this reassurance is well grounded. How can one have any reliable knowledge of another person's relationship with the transcendent? Can one be sure even in regard to himself when a transcendental relationship is involved? These questions are likely to be particularly persistent and sharp in areas where it is believed, as in orthodox Christianity, that man's relations with God depend not on man's intentions and powers but on God's. Who is man, that he should anticipate and announce the decisions of God? "Judge not, that ye be not judged." [1] The most dramatic symbol of God's nullification of human rank is the Crucifixion; the Lord of all mankind, according to this symbol, died ignominiously with two thieves on a desolate hillside.

In order to proceed with the discussion, however, let us set aside these doubts. Let us assume that excellence can be recognized. By whom? There is much sense in the notion that if there are absolutely superior men, no one can identify them but others of like superiority. To argue otherwise is to suggest some serious defect in the superior men, a defect manifest in their inability to recognize superiority in others. Thus, it is clear in Plato's plan for government by philosophers (those who have ascended to the Good) that the successor to a philosopher-king must be chosen by the philosopher-king himself. This is partly because Plato conceived of the philosopher as not only superior but perfect; hence no electorate composed of his inferiors could possibly have any grounds for challenging his judgment. But a similar logic works, although not quite so irresistibly, in an aristocracy where the leading class is con-

[1] Matthew 7:1.

ceived to be merely superior to all others without being perfect; the aristocrats' superiority tends to disqualify every competing source of power.

All of this is to say simply that the idea of a self-chosen elite, given elitist premises, is natural and logical.

The paradoxical idea is that of an elite chosen by their inferiors, and it is surprising that in the history of thought this idea is very old and has been supported by many distinguished thinkers. The main form of the idea is the principle that government is legitimate only with the consent of the governed. This principle was common both in ancient times and in the Middle Ages, long before the rise of modern democracy. It is true that it grew less out of confidence in popular judgment than out of the moral conviction that no one can be rightfully subjected to power without his own consent. But this conviction could not have been given any practical effect without some confidence in the good sense of the people. Thus a number of thinkers who believed in government by a superior few trusted sufficiently in the many to accord them the right of consent. The preeminent minority was to be identified, at least to the extent of being accepted, by the common majority.

How — that is, by what characteristics — can the superior few be identified? The most common answer out of the past is hard for most people now to take seriously. It is that the best are to be found among the wellborn. This was a very widespread belief during antiquity and the Middle Ages. Even John Locke, the principal theorist of modern liberalism, apparently assumed that government would generally be carried on by members of the hereditary aristocracy. That we find it difficult today to understand how men for so long could have accepted birth as a major sign of virtue or of capacity for governing testifies to the hold that democratic ideas have on our minds. But what sign is more reliable?

There are many possible answers to this question, but the main one offered by the modern world is undoubtedly "success." Excellence is indicated not by ancestry but by performance. There are many possible kinds of success — political, military, and academic, for example — but the kind most acclaimed in recent centuries has probably been that gained in business. As is well known, many early Calvinists believed that business success was a sign even of the kind of excellence prized by God.

Business success would not seem to be a very reliable sign of the kind of excellence needed for governing. In America, however, it has often been assumed that it is. This probably results from both America's esteem for businessmen and lack of esteem for politicians.

Do we in the latter half of the twentieth century, however, believe any more strongly in success than we do in good birth? Many of the best educated and most intelligent young people seem exceedingly cynical about business success. Many of them finally may seek it, but few seem likely to do so with the sense that thus they are testing and proving their human worth. As for political success, it is unlikely that many young Americans regard that as any more trustworthy a mark of personal superiority than having made a great deal of money in advertising or stocks. In general, those who have "made it" in almost any field are likely to be vilified as members of "the Power Elite" or "the Establishment."

If neither birth nor success is a reliable mark of excellence, however, by what criteria can we apportion power and honor? Many young people appear to evade this question through a kind of casual anarchism in which they assume that we do not need to apportion power and honor. But is this so? It can be argued that the shortest route to a system in which power is brutal and honor meaningless is by way of the assumption that neither power nor honor is needed. The tyrannies in Russia and China, for example, have arisen from a political philosophy postulating that the state is destined to "wither away." Undoubtedly it is well for students not to be taken in by the pretensions of the wellborn or the successful; but their insight leaves them facing the imposing question of how excellence can be recognized, and this is not far from being equivalent to the question of how society should be organized.

All of this has to do with the idea of inequality and its implications for the social order. Let us turn to the other side of the matter and ask about the implications of the idea of equality.

9

If human beings are essentially equal, are all conventional inequalities, such as those of wealth and social status, wrong?

The term "conventional" is used here as an antonym of the term "natural." Thus all inequalities resulting from the laws and customs of the social order are conventional; such inequalities include those not only of social status but also of power, wealth, and honor. Of course, it is possible to argue that in a good society the conventional inequalities would be natural as well. But if human beings are essentially, or naturally, equal, then all inequalities are purely conventional.

The idea that human beings are essentially equal, it is strange to say, had been a traditional tenet in the Western political mind for over a thousand years before it shaped up into a serious attack on conventional inequalities. Neither Stoics nor Christians sought to abolish even slavery, let alone other established ranks. This restraint came partly from their belief that nothing mattered except the state of one's soul and that this was not necessarily affected by one's rank in society. It stemmed also from their belief that the order of society was sanctioned by God and hence not to be attacked by men. The result was a social attitude somewhat disrespectful yet submissive. The inequalities inherent in the established order were at once condemned and tolerated — condemned because they were not in accord with the principle of equality and tolerated because of their ultimate insignificance and their dependence on divine permission.

However, as soon as it came to be thought that social conditions do affect the morals and the ultimate happiness of individuals, and, moreover, that social conditions are not determined and sanctified by God, the idea of equality began to shake and demolish the hierarchies of the established order. The idea was like a volcano, dormant so long that people had forgotten the fire and lava underneath and had built villages on its sides, and which suddenly began to erupt, pouring destruction on all the habitations around it.

Let me restate the logic of this event. If human beings are essentially equal, if the denial of their essential equality will not be compensated on another plane of being but does grave and irreparable harm, and if the social order is a product of man's will rather than God's, then privileges and power that cannot be justified in terms of the public good are intolerable. About two hundred years ago it began to seem that all of these conditions existed. The idea of equality was no longer dormant.

In the eruption that followed, the two principal thinkers, the volcanic figures of modern thought, were Rousseau and Marx. Both manifested a new sense that the individual's whole life and being are shaped by society; there is no transcendental soul or transcendental life, and in this sense the social order is man's total fate. Both thinkers, moreover, reflected the decline in the faith that society is governed by God and the growth of the conviction that there is nothing to alleviate worldly injustice or our responsibility for correcting it. These attitudes, combined with the idea of equality, moved both thinkers to challenge priests, kings, aristocrats, and (borrowing a phrase of Santayana's) all other "dominations and powers." We live today amid institutional ruins that Rousseau and Marx did much to produce, and we hear all around us the continuing reverberations of their assault on established institutions.

It is not hard to share their outrage. It is by no means clear that human beings are unequal in essence; at least it does not seem clear enough to justify the inequalities in wealth, power, and privilege that have prevailed in practically every society. Nor is it clear that even religious faith obliges us to acquiesce patiently in injustice. From the standpoint of faith, the rectification of injustice is no doubt a matter of less desperate and final importance than it is from a purely worldly standpoint. Nevertheless, religion does not imply a writing off of the world, and the idea that established injustice is always divinely sanctioned may be interpreted as the product of a particular religious culture and not a necessary inference from religion as such.

Thus whether one's basic stance is that of faith or of worldliness, it is not farfetched to see the subjection and deprivation suffered by the masses throughout history as a kind of continuing outrage perpetrated by the "respectable" elements heading society.

All the same, people do seem to be definitely unequal in important characteristics, such as intelligence and emotional balance, whether as a result of inequalities of essence or of inequalities of social condition. Furthermore, it seems indispensable that there be inequalities of power and rank within any effective social order; the abolition of all conventional inequalities does not appear to be compatible with the elementary requirements of human organization. For these reasons, even while feeling, with Rousseau and Marx, indignation over the inequalities that have been relentlessly imposed on the multitudes throughout history, one may draw back from the project of establishing total equality.

It is noteworthy that both Rousseau and some of the major followers of Marx have manifested an ambivalence of this kind. Both Rousseau and Marx stood for the general principle of radical democracy, government carried on either directly by the people or by representatives held closely responsible to the people. In drawing up actual governmental plans, however, as he did on one occasion for the government of Poland, Rousseau was willing to sanction marked inequalities of wealth, rank, and power. Some of Marx's followers have felt compelled to make even more far-reaching concessions of this kind. These have extended to the establishment and justification of what may be regarded as a new kind of class dictatorship.

This terrain of thought will be viewed from another vantage point when questions concerning power are discussed in the following chapter. Meanwhile, our present reflections may be brought to a close by pondering a question that draws together the subjects of these first two chapters, unity and equality. It is held by some thinkers that inequality is the primary form of estrangement; it is the most drastic kind of division, according to these thinkers, for some people to have power over others, for some to be wealthy while others are poor, and for some to be continually honored and flattered while others live under an everlasting shadow of neglect and disdain. These views suggest that estrangement might be conquered by doing away with inequality. Could this happen?

10

If all conventional inequalities were abolished,
would estrangement disappear?

This is one of the most important questions of the present time because it bears very closely on the problem of humanizing industrial society — of making a machine civilization considerate of the fragile, nonmechanical being of persons.

Traditional radicals and reformers, such as English socialists and American liberals, have seen the solution to the problem of industrial inhumanity in the idea of equality. The sharp lines between classes seemed to be the most inhuman aspect of industrialism. Not only did these lines separate people even more drastically than they had been separated under feudal and monarchical regimes; they seemed to delineate the basic situation which permitted industrialists to impose on the workers hours so long and wages so low that their lives reached depths of misery greater perhaps even than those experienced by most of the serfs and slaves of earlier ages. It was easy to conclude that the abolition of inequality would, in effect, be the conquest of estrangement.

The advance of industrialization, however, has cast doubt on this conclusion. One of the most bitter and persistent complaints in the highly industrialized societies has concerned, not class distinctions and inequities but personal alienation. Both the rich and the poor, it is said, make up a "lonely crowd," and the rich are about as lonely as the poor. It is tempting to say and it may be true that loneliness is far more bearable for the rich than for the poor. The fact remains that one of the major grievances of industrial man does not, on the face of it, concern the inequality that radicals and reformers have always taken to be the primary derangement of unreformed societies. This major grievance has concerned rather an estrangement which seems to affect the relations even of those who, economically, socially, and politically, are equal. Thus middle-class suburbanites in America apparently feel estranged, not particularly from the lower classes or the upper classes but from one another.

These conditions explain why we must ask whether the estrangement suffered today is traceable to the inequality attacked by traditional radicalism. As the above remarks suggest, there are two very different views on this matter. These call for a slightly more intensive examination on our part, for the future of industrial civilization is bound to depend heavily on our capacity to decide correctly between them.

Rousseau and Marx both represent the side of traditional radicalism. Both thinkers were acutely aware that something in modern life was weakening and severing the relationships of men to one another and to the physical world. Rousseau's *Confessions* is a poignant account of a lifetime of personal alienation; Marx's *Capital* could be described as a long, detailed analysis of the fragmentation of life wrought by capitalism. But the root of the matter, for both thinkers, was inequality — an inequality that was merely conventional and was not in accordance with the essence of man. Beneath the many estrangements men suffer is one great estrangement from which all the others grow, that between the few, who own most of the property and control the government, and the many, who own little or nothing and are the helpless subjects of an alien political power. As a consequence of this split, a communal and creative life is practically impossible — not only for the miserable multitudes but even for the rich and privileged, who are forced into a pampered and sterile defensiveness. The only way in which mankind can gain wholeness of life is by abolishing the distance between the few and the many.

In short, the conventional inequalities do not accord with underlying inequalities of essence. They are in violation of the nature of man and disruptive of genuine relationships. Doing away with these inequalities, therefore, is the main prerequisite for overcoming estrangement.

During the last century, however, there arose on the part of certain highly individual but profound and influential thinkers the very opposite notion, that by making men equal, we deepen estrangement. One of the earliest and greatest of these thinkers was the Danish religious philosopher, Søren Kierkegaard (1813–1855). The kind of estrangement that mattered most to Kierkegaard was estrangement from God.

This he thought was likely to be reinforced by equality. His argument was directed against what now is often called "mass society," that is, society in which individuality is censured and suppressed — not by the government alone but by a bigoted and inquisitorial populace, by "the masses." Kierkegaard's short essay *The Present Age* was an attack on conformity written long before such attacks became so fashionable as to be, in themselves, examples of conformity.

Kierkegaard was disturbed by what he saw as the disappearance of genuine individuals, of persons capable of passion and decision. Only individuals can be Christians, for authentic Christianity depends on the decision, setting one apart from all others, to base one's whole life on the Christian hope of eternal happiness. To be a Christian merely because everyone else is a Christian is, in truth, not to be a Christian at all. For Kierkegaard the leveling that seemed to be occurring everywhere around him manifested the movement of mankind into a state in which everyone was merely a passive reflection of everyone else. This was necessarily a movement away from Christianity.

In this sense, equality meant estrangement from God. Might one nevertheless be united with his fellow human beings? Not for Kierkegaard and not for anyone, probably, with an authentically religious viewpoint. Here we return to the theme of Question 4 in the preceding chapter. For those who believe in the possibility of a relationship with the transcendent, that relationship is prior to all others. The disruption of that relationship propels one into an isolation which is total, even though one may partially relieve the resultant anguish by behaving and thinking just like everyone else.

The other thinkers in whom the fading of the conventional inequalities inspired doubt or fear, rather than expectations of reunion, were in some ways quite different from Kierkegaard as well as being quite different from one another. For example, Alexis de Tocqueville (1805–1859) was interested primarily in the social and political consequences of equality and thought that these consequences could be discerned more clearly in the United States than anywhere else; thus his orientation was more historical than religious and his style, in contrast with

Kierkegaard's ardor and irony, was one of cool penetration. Nietzsche, as already noted, was an atheist; however, he felt a horror not unlike Kierkegaard's before the rising tide of equality. In the twentieth century, José Ortega y Gasset (1883–1955) was a cultivated Spanish philosopher who manifested little of Kierkegaard's faith in God, Tocqueville's interest in political institutions, or Nietzsche's hatred of Christianity, but in the spirit of all of them denounced "the revolt of the masses." These thinkers, with all of their idiosyncrasies, were at one in the conviction that equality presses the individual into conformity with the masses and thus alienates him from his own real nature. Someone who is alienated from himself cannot help but be alienated from others, even though he may in appearance be exactly like them. Paradoxically, then, as equality is attained, unity is lost.

This view is not necessarily conservative. The critics of mass society have not ordinarily made a central issue out of the preservation of traditional institutions or aristocratic rank. But all of them have refused to accept the common radical principle that doing away with the conventional inequalities will erase or even alleviate estrangement.

In what direction, then, should we move today? Radicals, although typically concentrating on class conflict, do not deny that estrangement has become more profound with the advance of industrialization. What they do deny, thus separating themselves definitively from the critics of mass society, is that any real equalization has come about in the process of this development. Under the egalitarian surface of things they see the same warfare of classes that Marx wrathfully delineated a century ago. Contemporary radicals therefore hold, with Rousseau and Marx, that we should move toward true equality.

Those on the other side, to their own disadvantage in public debate, do not agree among themselves on any single response to estrangement, nor do the various responses they suggest have the simplicity and clarity of the radical response. Many recommend that we treat inherited traditions and institutions with greater care and respect, although, as noted above, the critics of mass society are by no means uniformly or emphatically conservative. Others hope for the rise of new authorities and leaders. In general, however, it is probably true to say that their prevailing mood is strongly marked by historical resignation. That is, they see no completely reliable solution to the problem of estrangement and do not pretend to provide us with one. What they try to do, rather, is to illuminate our situation, thus preparing the individual to carry on a solitary life of resistance, in order both to salvage his own humanity and to be open to a future which may be far better than the present, and could even be resplendent, although it is a future beyond the scope of our foresight or control.

In concluding, let me suggest alternative lines of thought for those who would like to explore the possibilities without following the usual pathways either of radicalism or of conservatism. One of these lines of thought will probably appeal primarily to those of radical temperament. It begins in the idea that what is needed for overcoming estrangement is not just equality, pure and simple, but some particular kind of equality. What kind of equality? This is precisely the question that needs to be considered. That there is such a question was indicated by no less an authority than Marx himself when he warned against a kind of communism in which "the role of *worker* is not abolished, but is extended to all men." [2] From this vantage point one can see the possibility of a more subtle radicalism than, for example, the commonplace radicalism of many students today. Such a radicalism might free its followers from the tiresome compulsion, often in evidence among radical students, to show that the reality behind every undesirable situation is the exploitation of one class by another. It also might induce radicals to be less ready than they usually are to assume that any measure of equalization is bound to make life better.

The other line of thought begins in the idea that it is some particular kind of *inequality* that is needed for overcoming estrangement. Taking one's departure from this idea, one might hold a course clear both of conservatism and resignation, affirming the future as uncompromisingly as do radicals.

[2] Karl Marx, *Economic and Philosophical Manuscripts,* translated by T. B. Bottomore, in Erich Fromm, *Marx's Concept of Man* (New York: Frederick Ungar, 1961), pp. 124–125. The italics are Marx's.

One would reflect on the future, however, in terms of a new aristocracy. What kind of aristocracy? This, like the question above — what kind of equality? — is the question demanding reflection. Are scientists perhaps qualified to form a new aristocracy? Philosophers of some particular persuasion? Professors and students? Is the progress of technological society perhaps creating a technocracy or aristocracy of technicians? There are a multitude of possibilities, all implying that the task of the present is not equalization but the establishment of new "dominations and powers."

All that seems certain is that our situation is confusing, thus tempting us to flee to some of the mindless amusements and distractions our society liberally provides, but also that the situation is threatening, thus commanding us to think and to choose.

SUGGESTED READINGS

(Titles are listed chronologically. All are available in paperback or other inexpensive editions.)

Plato. *The Republic*
Aristotle. *Politics,* Books I and III–VI
Locke, John. *The Second Treatise of Government*
Rousseau, Jean Jacques. *Discourse on the Origin of Inequality*
Paine, Thomas. *The Rights of Man*
Tocqueville, Alexis de. *Democracy in America,* 2 vols.
Kierkegaard, Søren. *The Present Age*
Marx, Karl. *Capital,* Vol. I
Marx, Karl, and Engels, Friedrich. *Basic Writings on Politics and Philosophy.* Ed. by Lewis Feuer. (Doubleday)
Nietzsche, Friedrich. *Thus Spake Zarathustra*
Le Bon, Gustave. *The Crowd: A Study of the Popular Mind*
Ortega y Gasset, José. *The Revolt of the Masses*

4

Power

The discussion of unity and disunity and of equality and inequality brings us to an advantageous position from which to begin exploring the main subject of political science and thought, that is, power. Because men are disunited, power seems necessary for assuring order; because they are unequal, power seems justified as a way of placing everyone under the rule of the best human qualities. Many of the controversies of politics, moreover, have to do with the impact of power on unity and disunity and on equality and inequality. Thus power may be used both for separating men and for bringing them together, as is exemplified in policies of racial segregation and integration in America; it may support inequality, as when special tax benefits are accorded to the wealthy, and it may support equality, as is done in many countries through national systems of health care. Perhaps it would be impossible to use power so that it would neither divide nor unite, neither discriminate nor equalize.

It is because of these interconnections that the preceding two chapters have prepared us for reflecting on power.

Some of the most basic and difficult questions about power arise from its moral dubiousness. Perhaps power is essentially evil. At any rate, the use of power normally involves much evil: It tends to make those who possess it arrogant and it presupposes evil, as is evident in the conflicts that render order dependent on power. That human relations are pervaded by power is one of the most unmistakable signs of the radical imperfection of man.

Have even these few assertions, however, carried us too far, expressing certainty about matters that in fact are far from certain? Is it true, for example, that man is radically imperfect? And is power really indispensable? Some of the greatest and most idealistic men, such as the Russian novelist Leo Tolstoy, have answered both questions negatively and have called for the drastic curtailment or even the total elimination of power.

Here it seems we have encountered a question which demands an answer before we go any further. If politics is the use of power, clearly one of the first questions of political thought is whether power really is necessary.

11

Is there any source of order other than power?

The argument that there is a source of order other than power has been based, in the political thinking of the past, on at least three different ideas. One of these is that men are good and order is consequently spontaneous. John Locke, for example, in framing the philosophy of liberal government, assumed that human beings are fundamentally reasonable. This assumption meant, for Locke, that most people have the sense to see that others have certain rights, such as the right to life, simply because they are human beings. It meant also that most people are disposed to respect these rights. Locke saw men as having both the capacity and the inclination to live according to reason and the laws of nature. As a result, they depend on power only for overcoming certain deficiencies in the order that most of them spontaneously keep. They do not depend on it for creating order.

In sum, one source of order, other than power, is the reasonableness and the decency of man.

Another principle that has been put forward to show that order is not wholly dependent on power is natural harmony. Probably the clearest illustration of this view is the theory of the classical economists, a school of thought that flourished in the nineteenth century and provided what is still the basic belief-system of most supporters of "free enterprise." The classical economists did not regard men as good. On the contrary, they assumed that men were materialistic and self-seeking. But they did not conclude from this that order must be created and sustained with power. They believed that if governments would merely assure the main conditions of individual economic activity, such as security of property and stability of currency, but otherwise would not curb the freedom of people to seek profits in accordance with their own selfish promptings, good order would come into being naturally. The products most needed by society would be manufactured voluntarily; those making such products would be justly rewarded by the purchasers. On the other hand, those unable or unwilling to help meet the needs of society would lose out in the market and thus be automatically penalized. In this way, good order would arise from natural economic laws and with only a minimal application of human power. For the classical economists, order was contrived by what one of them called the "invisible hand" of the free market rather than by the visible hand of the government.

There are variations on this theme, such as the notion that the struggle among nations naturally conduces to the interests of all mankind. The idea underlying all such variations, however, is simply that laws of some sort inherent in the nature of things are the major source of order.

Finally, many thinkers have seen order as depending primarily on habit, custom, and tradition. They have not had to assume either the goodness of man or the harmony of nature in order to avoid dependence on power. Order rests rather on the human tendency to do what has always been done, to think what has always been thought, and to respect what is ancient. A society that is given a chance to develop peacefully will gradually build up an intricate structure of customs and traditions. This structure will contain more wisdom than any order deliberately designed and built at a particular time because it will be the work of a number of generations. Obviously, if the principle of human goodness is radical, because it leads naturally to a willingness to abandon established arrangements and restraints, the principle that order arises from habit and from loyalty to tradition is conservative.

Here, as the reader may have noticed, we have touched again on the views of Edmund Burke, discussed above in Question 3. According to these views, the major source of order is the habit-forming nature of man.

Anarchism is the idea that one of these forces — human goodness, natural harmony, or custom and tradition — or a combination of them, suffices for assuring order and that government therefore can be abolished. Typically, however, it is human goodness that anarchists count on, for the other sources of order contain an element of coercion. One who acts under the sway of natural forces or of habit is not fully free. Only if man is spontaneously orderly can the ancient conflict of order and freedom be resolved without compromise on either side.

A far more common position is that these three sources all are productive of some order but that they have to be supplemented with power. This is the position of liberals. They usually assume that men are fairly reasonable and decent but not perfect, that the laws of supply and demand can efficiently regulate some relationships but not the entire economy, and that custom and tradition contribute to social integration but do not alone assure it. Thus power is not the only source of order, and government can and must be limited. But no other sources of order, either singly or in combination, are sufficient, and power is therefore indispensable.

At the opposite pole from anarchism and liberalism is the view that man is irremediably disorderly. Every source of order, aside from power, is more or less ineffective. This view can be found in early Christianity, with its emphasis on original sin. It was held by Hobbes, for whom it was a logical outcome of the principle that human beings are essentially estranged. Its most notorious representative, however, is Niccolo Machiavelli (1469–1527).

Contrary to his lurid reputation, Machiavelli probably had

a somewhat less pessimistic view of man than either Augustine or Hobbes. He wrote often of the virtue and the corruption of peoples, thus showing that he did not consider human beings as wholly and always evil. Machiavelli saw virtue as consisting in qualities, such as loyalty and honesty, that predispose people to uphold order without being forced to do so; only when such qualities are lost, is absolute rule inevitable. Nevertheless, Machiavelli regarded all uncoerced and uncontrived order as highly unstable, and this was the heart of "Machiavellianism." Human beings tend always to be fickle and selfish, and are ingenious and tireless sources of chaos. Hence, order depends on the resolution and skill of political leaders. Machiavelli's two main works, *The Prince* and *The Discourses,* both consist wholly of reflections on the techniques and devices of political and military art. If there is a central teaching in Machiavelli, it is the political doctrine inherent in his pessimistic appraisal of man: Order and hence civilization rest not on human goodness but on the political sagacity of rulers.

Let me suggest another way of thinking about the whole question of whether there is any source of order other than power. This is by asking whether society determines the character of government, or vice versa. Currently, in universities, government is ordinarily looked at in the context of larger totalities, such as societies and historical eras. As one institution among many, government appears to be merely one element in an encompassing order and largely to be determined, in its character and policies, by that order. It is possible to reverse this relationship, however, and to see government as the center of thought and action from which the general character of society is determined. Those who desire swiftly to bring about some radical transformation of life are apt to look at things in this way.

From the first point of view, it is clear that power, or at any rate political power, is not the sole source of order; human beings create order spontaneously. From the second point of view, however, without the support of political artifice or force, society presumably would fall either into some lower form of order or into complete disorder. In this sense, political power underlies the highest forms of order, if not order itself.

The way in which one's view of human nature shapes without absolutely determining his political ideas can be clearly seen in connection with this question. If man is innocent and benign, there is no problem of order; human nature itself is the source of order. On the other hand, to say that man is selfish and cruel is to say that he is naturally disorderly, and one has to ask how this tendency can be counteracted.

These matters are not so simple, however, that one need only deduce political conclusions from psychological premises. In the present instance, for example, the notion that man is selfish and cruel must, it is true, prompt one to consider government as a possible source of order; it must at the same time, however, prompt one to fear what man in his selfishness and cruelty may do when armed with the power of government. Thus easy, one-step deductions are barred and simple patterns of thought are untenable. One is compelled to ask, for example, whether any human beings are exceptions to the general depravity of human nature, and, if so, whether it would be possible or desirable to give them total power. If he answers either question negatively, then he is led to ask, more realistically, whether the consequences of human depravity can be somehow counteracted among those who govern.

The point, however, is that such reasoning is ordinarily carried out under the dominating influence of a concept of man. That concept may of course be altered in the course of one's reflections. But it remains a touchstone of political doctrine.

The issue marked out by anarchism, liberalism, and Machiavellianism is forced on us today by the disorder in the world and in American society. The hatred and confusion filling Africa, Asia, and Latin America, the revolt of American blacks against white domination, and the disruptive acts of radical students, all make it clear that order cannot be taken for granted. Does order among nations today depend on the incomprehensibly expensive and destructive armed forces of the United States? Does order within the United States require that the police be freed from procedural rules that safeguard individuals but perhaps inhibit the suppression of crime?

As these questions indicate, in asking whether there can be any order aside from that created and sustained with power, we are asking to what degree life can be free and cooperative.

This is a basic and difficult question. Still, it is only one of several such questions put before us by the fact of power. To begin with, as soon as it is concluded that power cannot be eliminated from human associations, the question arises as to its effects on those who wield it. Does it in some way enhance their humanity — for example, by enabling them to be benefactors? Or is it apt to corrupt them? Does it make for happiness, or is it simply a burden?

12

Does power make the lives of its possessors better, or worse?

Two answers that are diametrically opposed to one another, both of which come down to us from antiquity, can serve to dramatize the issue. For Aristotle, politics constituted a particularly favorable sphere for the realization of one's full humanity. When Aristotle said that "man is a political being," he meant in part that through political activity one can actualize all of his potentialities. Men are essentially united in the sense that man's essence, as expressed in virtues like courage, pride, and truthfulness, can be realized only by means of human relationships. The sum of all relationships is the state (or, more precisely, the *polis*) in that the state embraces and harmonizes all lesser groups. Hence, to become comprehensively related to one's fellow human beings requires conscious participation in the affairs of state, that is, in politics. This is roughly the logic of Aristotle's position. To put it very briefly, Aristotle saw the possession of power, in company with other citizens, as providing incomparable amplitude of life.

It is to be noted that Aristotle was thinking both of virtue and of happiness. In modern times many people have regarded these as antithetical. For Aristotle, they were indivisible. Political activity was at once duty and fulfillment.

It is also to be noted, however, that Aristotle's views would apply only to political activity carried on in a good state. Aristotle saw no virtue or happiness in being, or supporting, a tyrant. True political activity is possible only in the environment created by self-government and the rule of law.

Aristotle's attitude has been shared in our own day by many public figures and by many observers of public life. It has often been argued, for example, that the American presidency provides an unusually favorable sphere for bringing out the idealism and ability of its occupants and that the office tends to enhance the stature of those who hold it. Harry Truman is often used to illustrate this point. He entered the presidency as an apparently commonplace and even frightened person but learned to act with a decisiveness and acumen sufficient for many to rank him among the greater American presidents.

A completely different position from that of Aristotle was taken by another great thinker of antiquity, Epicurus (342?– 270 B.C.). Epicurus' viewpoint was summed up in the injunction, "Live unknown." Epicurus was trying to deal with a general disorientation of life, not unlike the "alienation" of the present time, that came about with the passing of the city-state as a viable form for human life. In a world that suddenly seemed vast and strange, Epicurus wished to discover how one might attain self-sufficiency and serenity. He was led, in this search, to repudiate the notion that "man is a political being." Politics means the very opposite of the good life; it means continuous vexation, dependence on others. Only in private life — a kind of tomb in the eyes of Aristotle — can one find happiness and independence.

Today, an Epicurean observer of American life would say that the multitudes who seek political office, trying to climb from state and local posts up to the summits of the federal government in Washington, are very foolish, for they will find only annoyance and anguish. Equally, however, he would condemn campus militants and activists, for they violate the rule of detachment no less than do the members of the Establishment whom they attack. An Epicurean would not be likely to sympathize even with the common exhortations to vote. One should concentrate on maintaining balance and peace in his own personal life, regardless of the political conditions surrounding him.

Aristotle and Epicurus define either end of a wide range of possible answers to the question of whether power tends to make the lives of its possessors better or worse. Probably most

Americans today would be unwilling to endorse either position. Many of them would probably say that wielding power may not improve one's life in the sense of bringing fulfillment and happiness but that it is a duty and thus at least must tend to make one's life morally better. A position roughly of this kind was developed by the Stoics a century or more after the time of Epicurus, and it contributed to the kind of political resolution that was needed to administer and defend the Roman Empire.

For the Stoics, the conception of the universe as a divine order dictated the conscientious performance of the duties of one's station; one should play his part, whatever the part. Thus political office should not be sought. If one is a slave he should accept his lot; one should realize that his humanity cannot be taken from him by his enslavement but only by his failure to fulfill his duties with a rational and imperturbable awareness that thus he participates in the divine order of the cosmos. But if one finds himself faced with political tasks, then he should perform them without being swayed by the uncertainties and discouragements that are apt to assail a conscientious person in a position of power; whatever consequences ensue from one's actions, all is as it should be.

Whether or not this outlook is correct, it has to be admitted that so austere an emphasis on duty might well prove useful in times of political trouble. Rome found it so and perhaps the time is coming when America will as well.

Of course the old commonplace that "power tends to corrupt" has a bearing on this question. Most Americans would probably agree with this commonplace as fully as they would with the principle recommending the duty of public service. But if power tends to corrupt, then it tends to make one morally worse; if it does that, then it must tend to make one's life worse, even though it may make it more exciting or more pleasurable.

These three attitudes, the Aristotelian, the Epicurean, and the Stoic, all are relatively hopeful and constructive. The Epicurean and Stoic attitudes reflect great disillusionment, but they purport nevertheless to show man how he can live well in spite of the mountainous evils surrounding him. Note should also be taken, however, of a more cynical view — one that is likely, in times as disturbed as ours, to have numerous adherents. Power may not be morally or socially beneficial, according to this view, but it is eminently worth having, either for the opportunities it provides for a ruthless and unsentimental person to satisfy his own interests, or merely for the pleasure and exhilaration of wielding it. One does not expect to find such an attitude argued by philosophers but rather merely reflected in the lives of men who are too fully occupied with gaining and using power to have time for thinking and writing. What is perhaps its sole appearance in the writings of a great thinker is by no means blatant.

Machiavelli was not indifferent either to the ends sought by men of power or to the inherent morality of the means they employed. Success was not everything for Machiavelli. He was, however, deeply fascinated with power, so much so that he often evinced satisfaction with an adroit political maneuver and showed relatively little concern either with its ultimate consequences or its inherent morality. Moreover, the charm of power seems to have been enhanced, in Machiavelli's eyes, when it assumed some of its more violent and terrifying forms. Thus, while Machiavelli did not explicitly defend the idea that power is an end in itself, much less the idea that it is a means for satisfying the private interests of the one who wields it, his writings do sometimes express the feeling that power is in some measure justified simply by the glory and excitement of political virtuosity.

The question of whether power tends to make the lives of its possessors better or worse is an important one today. The politics of the twentieth century has been filled with confusion and violence. As the preceding discussion has brought out, it is far from clear that having power in any era is beneficial to those who have it. Having power in our era appears, at least so far as happiness and morality are concerned, a particularly dubious privilege. Thus politics is likely to repel many of the most sensitive and honorable people; at the same time and for the same reasons, it is likely to attract some of the most insensitive and unscrupulous. Clearly a situation of this kind constitutes a crisis in the political order. Apart from all other factors tending to lower the moral level of the public realm, demoralization itself tends, by repelling the best and attracting the worst, to produce further demoralization. How far these remarks apply to various present-day societies will be disputed; that they have some application, however, scarcely seems in doubt. This is why the question before us is important. If the best people refuse to become involved in the political order, is it not reasonable to suppose that that order is doomed?

Now let it be assumed that, reflecting on the first two questions of this chapter, we have become convinced both of the practical necessity of power and of the moral legitimacy of wielding it. What about those underneath? Why should they submit?

13

Why obey?

To possess power is, at least superficially, honorable and glorious. To be without power, however, and subject to the power of others is at least superficially degrading. Why should one accept such a position? This is one of the central questions in the whole history of political thought, for if it cannot be answered, then the entire political order with all of its offices, laws, and dignities is indefensible.

Another way of posing the question would be to ask what can make power legitimate or what can turn it from mere naked force into authority. Probably in all times human beings have been offended by stark power, by a demand for obedience unsupported by any reference to moral right. It is also probable that not very much has been required to overcome this feeling of offense; disobedience is dangerous, and some quite fragile claim to legitimacy may suffice to reconcile most people to subordination. Nevertheless, it is not just a handful of radicals or of peculiarly conscientious people, such as Quakers, who are capable of asking why obedience is owed to a government. The self-respect of practically all human beings depends on assurance that the government they obey has a moral right to be obeyed.

Probably the oldest and most durable answer to the question, why obey, is one that today seems absurd: the divine right of kings. Until just a few centuries ago most governments claimed that that their power was given to them by God. This claim was made well before the rise of Christian societies. "From the beginning of history," writes the historian Christopher Dawson, "the king has been distinguished from the tyrant, the magistrate or the official by the possession of a *charisma* or divine mandate which sets him apart from other men." [1] One of the main inferences drawn from this principle was, of course, the rule of absolute obedience. Political resistance was rebellion against the divine.

The concept of the divine right of kings, however, may strike one as an effort not so much to answer the question as to stifle it. Power entails an immense moral strain for those subject to it, as noted above, and it is not surprising that in religious ages men tried to relieve this strain by conceiving of power as divinely sanctioned. The idea of divine right, nevertheless, is thoroughly irrational, not primarily because it is based on a religious premise, but because from the premise — that God is — the conclusion does not follow. The idea that God has sanctified every government is no more necessitated by religious faith than is the idea that God has sanctified every revolution. Perhaps it is not unreasonable to think that one element in the durability of the idea that kings rule by divine right is the desire of governing classes to suppress an explosive question. Certainly the idea was not reached by open-minded inquiry and could not long withstand such inquiry.

A complete change of mind has apparently occurred in recent centuries. Worldliness and religious skepticism have rendered the principle of divine right wholly implausible, and the ideal of personal freedom has shifted the burden of proof, in questions of obedience, decisively over to the side of the government. At the same time, the rising self-confidence and political awareness of the multitudes have given to disobedience revolutionary, history-making potentialities. Thus the

[1] Christopher Dawson, *Religion and Culture* (New York: Meridian Books, 1948), p. 109.

question, why obey, has been asked with mounting insistence and portentousness. Today in America, for many principled and intelligent people, the presumption that government is to be respected and obeyed has disappeared almost completely, and disobedience has taken on the aura of a virtue.

The simplest defense of obedience, aside from the theory of divine right, may be that contained in the idea of consent. As Locke put it, "Men being . . . by Nature, all free, equal and independent, no one can be put out of this Estate, and subjected to the Political Power of another, without his own *Consent*." [2] Thus one is not obliged to obey unless he has voluntarily agreed to do so. At one point, at least, Locke seems to imply that not only does the founding of a government require consent but that every governmental act significantly affecting one's life or rights requires consent, for he writes that "the *Supream Power cannot take* from any Man any part of his *Property* without his own consent." [3] If this injunction were literally followed, payment of taxes would be voluntary. Indeed, if one is under no obligation to obey unless he consents to do so in each particular case, then strictly speaking he is under no obligation to obey at all.

The theory that political obligation is based on consent represents a drastic subordination of government to freedom. Even assuming that Locke did not mean to go so far as to require consent for every particular governmental act, the general thrust of the theory is that nothing should be demanded of an individual that does not accord with his uncoerced and fully conscious will. It is not surprising that some political thinkers sought to formulate a doctrine of obedience with less anarchistic overtones. The result is as clearly represented as anywhere in the theory of the "general will," which was definitively formulated by Rousseau, although it had been implicit in a number of political philosophies, such as those of Plato and Aristotle.

According to this theory, the obligation to obey does not depend on a prior act of consent (although it happens that

[2] John Locke, *Two Treatises of Government,* ed. by Peter Laslett (Cambridge: University Press, 1960), p. 348. The italics are Locke's.

[3] *Ibid.,* p. 378. The italics are Locke's (as is the spelling of "supreme").

Rousseau did incorporate the idea of consent in his political theory). A government deserves to be obeyed if its commands conform to what Rousseau called the general will. What is the general will? Or, to put the question in a more convenient form: Owing to what quality or qualities is a will general? Not owing simply to its being the will of everyone, although this was part of it for Rousseau, for this would make the theory of the general will only another form of the theory of consent.

Rousseau explicitly distinguished between "the will of all" and the general will, and asserted that there is often a great difference between them. The will of all, he wrote, is "no more than a sum of particular wills." [4] The distinctive quality of the general will, according to Rousseau, is that it "considers only the common interest." [5] For a will to be general, then, it must be directed toward the good of everyone. It is not necessary here to ask whether, in any conceivable circumstances, there can be a truly common good, a value shared equally by every member of a society. This possibility depends on whether, in answer to Question 1 in this book, human beings are essentially at one. The main point here is that according to the theory of the general will a government has a legitimate claim to obedience only when its commands represent the true, ultimate interests of all of the people.

Rousseau's acknowledgment that the people are subject to error, so that the will of all is not necessarily the general will, has led to the idea that a single ruling person, even an absolute dictator, might represent the general will. Accordingly, writers have claimed to see in regimes such as Lenin's or Hitler's a Rousseauean spirit. This, however, is based on a misreading of Rousseau. In spite of all the complexities of *The Social Contract*, Rousseau's own words seem quite conclusive. "The general will," he wrote, "to be really such, must be general in its object as well as its essence; . . . it must both come from all and apply to all." [6] Thus while the will of the people may be

---

[4] Jean Jacques Rousseau, *The Social Contract and Discourses*, translated with an introduction by G. D. H. Cole (New York: E. P. Dutton and Co., 1950), p. 26.

[5] *Ibid.*, p. 26.

[6] *Ibid.*, p. 29.

mistaken, a will directed toward the common good is not the general will unless it also is the will of the people.

Rousseau was not so unrealistic as to demand unanimity in every decision, however. Thus he did not intend readers to take him literally when he said that the general will must "come from all." He was willing to accept majorities of varying size, with the size depending on circumstances, as surrogates for "all." This seems reasonable enough. However, it opens up the possibility of an inference that is startling but quite important for understanding the theory of the general will. This is, that in obeying the general will even when one disagrees with it, or, more accurately, believes that the will he is forced to obey is not the general will, one is free. Obedience and freedom, usually assumed to be diametrically opposed to one another, are in these circumstances identical. How can this be? The answer is logical. A person is free, presumably, when he does what he really wants to do, and it may be assumed in turn that what he really wants to do is to realize his own ultimate good. He does that, however, in obeying the general will. The conclusion is inescapable: In obeying the general will he is free. This would be true even if he felt threatened or crushed by that will.

The purpose of setting forth this inference so starkly is to make the basic theory clear, not to induce the reader to reject it. If the theory should be rejected at all, it should be done only after careful reflection, for the whole issue is exceedingly complicated and difficult.

The main problem presented by the question of obedience is the reconciliation of obedience with liberty. "To renounce liberty," as Rousseau asserted, "is to renounce being a man." [7] But it is of the essence of government that it demands obedience and thus, apparently, a renunciation of liberty. How then can even the best government mean anything but that the humanity of those under it is fatally abridged? Anarchists claim that it cannot. The theories of consent and the general will, on the other hand, both attempt to justify government by showing how one can obey and still be free. The principal

[7] *Ibid.*, p. 9.

difference between the two theories is this: One of them conceives of freedom only in terms of conscious will and tries to legitimize obedience by tracing it back to an act of consent; the other conceives of freedom in terms of a will that may not be fully conscious (a person willing his own welfare may not know what political measures will promote that welfare). Thus the theory of the general will maintains that a law that does not rest on explicit consent may yet command what contributes to the individual's real good and thus enhance his freedom.

Both theories involve serious difficulties. The theory of consent is simple and comprehensible on the surface, but it is hard to see how it could be put into practice. It cannot mean that the legitimacy of every governmental command depends on a separate act of consent; this would be incompatible with stable, effective government. Thus, it must mean that the legitimacy of each governmental command follows from some prior act of consent. The trouble is that rarely is a command, such as a law or executive order, so supported; people are not normally related to the governments over them by acts of clear and specific consent. In reading Locke, one can easily sense the embarrassment this difficulty causes him. In a passage concerning taxation he asserts that when property is taken from a citizen, it must be "with his own Consent, *i.e.*, the Consent of the Majority." [8] Thus individual consent is equated with majority consent. But there is no manifest justification for doing this, and it merely presents the question of obedience in a more specific form: Why obey the majority? In another passage, Locke asserts that one tacitly consents to a government merely by traveling freely on its roads or even by simply being within its territory.[9] Judged by this standard, however, the most despised tyrannies have rested on the consent of the governed.

A further question that arises is this: Is one bound by consent that one has given because of his ignorance or confusion and that one should not have given? Was a young German who swore allegiance to Hitler when he first came to power in

[8] Locke, *op. cit.*, p. 380.
[9] *Ibid.*, p. 366.

1933 morally obliged to obey every command of the Nazi government? These are just a few of the questions provoked by the theory of consent.

The theory of the general will implies, on the other hand, that one might, as stated in a notorious phrase of Rousseau's, be "forced to be free." One might be free in doing, under the supervision of the police, something that he does not at all want to do. One might even be free in prison. Hegel argued that a criminal really wills his own punishment; this concept suggests the possibility of arguing that a government wisely and justly carrying out its penal responsibilities liberates people by locking them up. This idea is not at all nonsensical (any more than it is nonsensical to speak of a criminal as being enslaved by an evil will). But it is an idea that gives one pause. Is there perhaps some dangerous sophistry concealed in thus equating force and freedom?

Both theories, that of consent and that of the general will, can be extremely puzzling; after trying to think them through, one may wonder whether it was really worth raising the issue. In truth, however, the issue can hardly be suppressed. To obey unconditionally, that is, to obey always and as a matter of course, means nothing less than the abandonment of selfhood; the center of choice and responsibility is shifted from the self to the one who commands. It is probably a vague sense that the stakes are so high that makes almost everyone wish for some kind of assurance that the government to which he is subject is legitimate. It would be literally bestial never to inquire why one is obliged to obey.

The necessity for reflecting on the duty of obedience is even more firmly established, however, if we note that it also would be bestial persistently or capriciously to refuse to obey. Civilization itself depends on obedience being normal and disobedience being exceptional; otherwise the fundamental order, which offers the possibility of civilized life, would break down. It follows that those ostensibly liberated and radical spirits who disobey frequently and thoughtlessly are as irresponsible as the slavish spirits who obey invariably and unquestioningly.

Regardless of which theory is accepted — and probably every theory of obedience is some form either of the theory of consent or of the theory of the general will — one is then faced with a somewhat more concrete question. What kind of government meets the requirements of one's theory? If the duty of obedience must be derived from consent, what rulers or what forms of rule deserve consent? If the duty of obedience must be derived from the general will, what sort of governing arrangements are likely most effectively to bring forth the general will?

14

Who should rule?

"Anyone" and "no one" are both among the answers that have been given to this question, as implausible as they may, at first glance, appear to be.

The answer "anyone" is implicit in the philosophy of Hobbes. One reason why Hobbes was willing that anyone should rule was his somewhat cynical egalitarianism. Hobbes had no faith in great men or in aristocracies; no one was exempted from his pessimistic appraisal of man. Therefore, he did not feel that it much mattered who ruled. Looking at things so pessimistically, however, could he not just as well have argued that no one should rule? No, for he thought this would result in intolerable chaos. This position of course makes some sense if, as Hobbes believed, human beings are essentially estranged.

Still, if one wished to pursue the point, one could ask whether intolerable chaos might not also result from giving command to a specimen of Hobbesian humanity, a person invariably and uncompromisingly egotistical, who is merely a complex material object governed like the rest of reality by the laws of cause and effect. Hobbes thought not. His reasoning was roughly as follows: What each one, in his egotism, desires above everything else is self-preservation; self-preservation can be gained only where there is peace; peace is the product of a strong, well-ordered state. Such a state is thus a primary goal on the part of the subjects of a ruler. What does the ruler desire? Like everyone else, he desires self-preservation. In his case, however, the primary condition for fulfilling this desire is power. How is power to be obtained? Through organizing a strong, well-ordered state — the same end that is sought by his subjects. There is thus a fundamental identity of interest between government and people.

On these grounds Hobbes thought that any man in command of a state would be about as effective as any other and would try to further, albeit for his advantage, the interest of his subjects.

On the other side, mistrust of power, of course, is common. Only a few thinkers, however, and those relatively obscure, have brought themselves to the extreme view that no one should be entrusted with power. These thinkers, as the reader may realize from an earlier discussion, are anarchists. They are pessimistic in their conviction that power will inevitably be misused. They are optimistic, however, in believing that it can be dispensed with and that order and peace can be securely established without any coercion at all. Every form of power, to them, is both intolerable and useless. How can intelligent people affirm so self-contradictory a theory?

They affirm it only by maintaining, in one way or another, that the misdeeds of those who govern do not reflect the essential nature of man. Man in his essence is cooperative and unselfish, they say. This will be revealed when governments have been destroyed or perhaps when civilization has further evolved. On suppositions of this sort anarchists have built, in compensation for the crimes and terrors which many of them have experienced in their own lives, a daring hope: Oppression and government itself will die away and humanity will become a perfect community. This hope may strike one as strange and implausible. But it has generated a doctrine that has appealed to men of great stature, such as Tolstoy, and that has a moral purity and a philosophical audacity commanding respect.

When we consider the answers lying in between these two extremes we cross a path which we followed in the preceding chapter. We encounter issues connected with inequality and equality. Speaking very broadly, the question of who should rule has been thrashed out by two political and philosophical parties. These are the supporters of the few and the supporters of the many. A reasonable decision in favor of one side or the other can be made only after reflecting on whether human beings are essentially equal or not.

Are there certain virtues, attainable by a few but not by the majority, that render those possessing them deserving of power? It has frequently been claimed that there are. Philosophical wisdom was held by Plato to be such a virtue; the sanctity supposedly inherent in ecclesiastical ordination has been so regarded by both Catholics and Protestants; and unique political capacities have often been attributed to some minority distinguished by family background, military achievement, or business success. Indeed, human beings show a surprisingly strong inclination to exalt some minority or other. The medieval priests and kings may have been deposed, but the twentieth century has raised up its own priestly and royal authorities, as is evident in the trust that has been placed in Communist and Nazi elites as well as in scientists, technicians, and managers.

Recently, however, many young people apparently have become profoundly mistrustful of every minority with power. Leaders in business, in government, in the churches, and in the universities all have been vociferously condemned. The general principle aimed against them has been that no one should rule but the people themselves.

The idea of popular rule has received less support in the history of political thought than one might expect. It is certain that twenty-five hundred years ago in Greece many people believed in what today is often called "participatory democracy," for a number of the city-states were direct (rather than representative) democracies. The great Greek thinkers, however, treated democracy either with scorn or with definite reservations. The conquests of Alexander the Great, several centuries before the time of Christ, largely extinguished democracy, which has only revived in recent times. In the interim there were democratic movements, and people here and there believed in democracy. But political thinkers, while often granting a significant measure of authority to the people in theory, usually seemed to assume that this authority in practice would be subject to severe limitations; practically never did they seem to envision or desire actual popular rule.

Whether the dearth of democratic thought was owing to the class bias of those who had the leisure to think and to write, to a wisdom that enabled them to discern the insufficiencies of democracy, to the difficulties of organizing popular rule prior to the development of technological media of communication, or to some other cause, is uncertain. In any case it was not until the seventeenth and eighteenth centuries that the ideal of democracy was clearly and uncompromisingly affirmed. Rousseau was the first great thinker in whose writings this occurred. For Rousseau, man is deprived of his humanity by having to live under a government in which he has no part. This diminishment of man would take place even if the government were benevolent and wise. It would be unlikely, if a great number of people were excluded from participation, that the government would be anything but selfish and oppressive. Rousseau attributed to the people, so far as they are neither corrupted by modern urban civilization nor frustrated by defective political arrangements, a quality it is hardly too strong to term "sanctity."

Is it really any more sensible, however, to rest confidence in great numbers than in some select minority? Do the doubts that most political philosophers have had about popular rule constitute a kind of consensus of the wise, a consensus we should be hesitant to contradict? The modern experience with democracy and socialism, through which the people have gained more if not all power, has prompted many misgivings. Numerous observers have judged the cultural tastes of the people to be crude and their political opinions to be based on ignorance and prejudice.

It can be argued in response that the people in reality have gained little power and that their failings reflect the irresponsible influence still wielded by minorities such as the commercial interests dominating television and press.

Obviously it is hard not to vacillate between the few and the many. This is why many thinkers, from the earliest periods of political thought, have refused to advise that either the few alone or the many alone be entrusted with power and have argued that in some fashion both together should govern. Aristotle thought that such a sharing of power could be accomplished by granting power to a large middle class. Rule by this class, he held, was likely to be more moderate and sensible than rule either by an aristocracy or by the populace.

Where a strong middle class does not exist, Aristotle's advice is inapplicable, of course, for such a class cannot be created easily or quickly and perhaps cannot be created at all. Also, some people feel that while neither the upper class nor the lower class should govern alone, each should share in power. Accordingly, political thinkers have given much attention to organizational devices whereby aristocracy and democracy might be combined. It has more than once been suggested, for example, that the executive should be reserved for persons of special distinction while the legislature should express the will of the people.

A list of the great thinkers who have urged a combination of the few and the many would be an impressive collection of names. This fact and the arguments discussed above suggest that there is wisdom in the idea. There is one objection to it, however, that for many will be conclusive: It contains little promise of the radical social and political renewal which today is called for by many students and intellectuals. Where all classes share in governing, nothing is likely to be done that seriously jeopardizes the interests of any class. Hence the ideal of government that is neither by the few nor the many, but is mixed, is apt to appeal only to those who are too satisfied or else too discouraged to look toward the future with high expectations.

Often it is those with high expectations who pose the question most dramatically. They are the ones most likely to claim that some particular group is not merely the best of the alternatives as a repository of power but that it can redeem mankind from the vicissitudes and agonies of history. Plato made this claim for philosophers, Marx for the proletariat, and Lenin for the Communist Party. When faced with claims of this kind, one has to ask how much can reasonably be expected of rulers. Should we be satisfied with prudence on the part of our leaders and with a conduct of affairs that avoids disaster? Or should we look for redeeming wisdom, for a Moses to lead us out of our captivity within commonplace life and mediocre visions?

A final general question concerning power deserves our attention. There is little doubt that the modern answer to the question of who should rule is, on the whole, that the many should rule. The power of an aristocratic institution, like the Supreme Court in the United States, indicates that this answer is not unqualified. Most defenders of minority powers and privileges, however, see such institutions as merely prudent restraints on what is predominantly and properly government by the people. Few openly attack the basic principle of popular rule. In these circumstances it is appropriate that we consider how popular government best can be carried on.

15

If the people rule, is it better that they do so directly or through representatives?

Many present-day students feel strongly that direct (or "participatory") democracy is far superior to representative democracy. Their sentiments seem to be those expressed by Rousseau when he stated flatly that "sovereignty . . . cannot be represented" and when he added his famous animadversion on the English political system. "The people of England," he asserted, "regards itself as free: but it is grossly mistaken: it is free only during the election of members of parliament. As soon as they are elected, slavery overtakes it, and it is nothing." [10]

Perhaps this view is valid. Considering the fervor and frequency with which the case for participatory democracy is made, however, it might be well for us to note that the case on the side of representative democracy is not insubstantial. The following four arguments are probably the strongest and most common points making up that case.

1. The representative system makes it possible, while allowing the people as a whole to have the final word, to empower those who stand out for their intelligence, their experience, and their interest in political matters. Direct democracy tends to submerge such minorities in the masses.

[10] Rousseau, *op. cit.*, p. 139.

2. Representatives of the people can devote all of their time to government, whereas the people as a whole cannot. The consequence, since government must be carried on continuously, is that representative democracy can provide steadier popular control of day-to-day government than can direct democracy. Even in a very small state, the entire populace could not be expected to assemble oftener than once every few weeks. Thus most of the time government must be carried on by unsupervised minorities.

3. A representative body provides better opportunities for leisured, unemotional deliberation than does a great popular assembly. Representatives are in daily, face-to-face contact, so that their antipathies toward one another may be tempered by personal understanding; also, being few in number and meeting frequently, their relationships can readily be structured by formalities that protect the spirit and the processes of deliberation. Members of large multitudes, on the other hand, cannot for the most part be personally acquainted; the presence of a crowd in itself is incompatible with deliberation and is an incitement to inflammatory speech; and great numbers are more likely than the few making up a representative body to be carried away by some momentary emotion.

4. Direct democracy is only workable in polities that are very small, both in population and in area; otherwise, frequent assemblies of the people are impossible. Representative democracy opens the way to large-scale and even to global political integration. This may have advantages beyond the obvious one of linking together large numbers of people, with all of the military, economic, and cultural gains that would become available. A polity may, for example, as James Madison argued in the famous "Federalist No. 10," embrace such a great variety of interests that it would be difficult for any one faction, such as a racial or economic minority, to gain ascendancy and act in opposition to the public interest.

These four points constitute a sober and sensible case for representative democracy. Indeed, it is doubtful that proponents of direct democracy can present a case for their side that is equally sober and sensible. This is not to say that their position is weaker than that of the proponents of representative democracy but rather that it is a position of another kind.

Those who argue for representative democracy usually stand on the ground of common sense; this means, among other things, that they expect man in the future to be what he has ordinarily been in the past, a being who *en masse* does not usually manifest either acute intelligence or a firm sense of responsibility. On the other hand, those who argue for direct democracy commonly seem to place more reliance on hope than on experience, on what man might become than on what he has usually been.

At least two compelling visions inspire the ideal of direct democracy; it is unlikely that either of these will give way or even be much weakened by objections brought forth by common sense.

First, there is the vision of the individual as governing his own life — not merely in the negative and partial sense of having a sphere in which he can behave as he likes but rather in the positive and complete sense of deliberating over and deciding the whole order of his existence. The individual alone cannot be sovereign in this way. But direct democracy allows him to share in sovereignty, and where there is a large measure of agreement binding together the governing populace he may feel that the decisions of the people are in effect his own personal decisions. In contrast, representative democracy means passive citizenship. As Rousseau asserted, one is free when he votes, but at other times he is a subject rather than a sovereign.

Beyond this, there is a vision of community that cannot be accommodated within the concept of representative democracy. Representation modifies but does not overcome that deep and drastic division between those who have power and those who do not, between government and governed. Few other circumstances so alienate human beings from one another. An enduring and powerful source of appeal on the side of direct democracy is that it promises to do away with this noxious division; no longer will mankind be divided between rulers and ruled. A direct democracy could be, fully and literally, a community.

Thus, matching the practicality of one side is the imagination of the other. How can a choice be made? Pondering the following questions might help one in defining his position:

1. How much of one's time is politics worth? Rousseau as-

serted that "the better the constitution of a State is, the more do public affairs encroach on private in the minds of citizens." [11] Direct democracy places heavy demands on the time and attention of everyone, and it is doubtful that one can logically favor this system unless he believes that politics should be man's primary concern.

2. Is it possible for industrial societies to get along without bureaucracy? If so (as Marx, for example, seemed to believe), then direct democracy may sometime be made to work. If not, then the ideal of direct democracy is probably a delusion. If bureaucracy is inevitable, one of the overriding problems of politics is that of rendering it responsible to the whole society. This is more likely to be accomplished by representatives, possessing a measure of expertise and meeting continuously, than by a miscellaneous assemblage of the people meeting only now and then.

3. On what human quality does the solution of political problems primarily depend? If on expertise, direct democracy is a dubious ideal; if on common sense, then it may be defensible. The question, clearly, is how specialized and rare the necessary quality is.

The whole issue reflects man's efforts to reconcile power and his own dignity. The general idea of democracy is that to do this, sovereignty or ultimate power must be held by the people. But how is this possible? "Government by the people," literally, would not be government. The concepts of representative and direct democracy are two different ways of grappling with this problem. Representative democracy is the "realistic" solution in that it acquiesces in the inevitability of government, of concentrated power, and merely demands that those who exercise this power do so subject to periodic, formal approval by the people. Direct democracy is the "idealistic" solution. It moves a long way toward anarchism; government is reduced to a subordinate administrative apparatus and the people are expected themselves to pass the laws which the administration is to carry out. Representative democracy does not overcome the alienation of government and governed, but

[11] *Ibid.*, p. 93.

it can be said in its defense that it does not try to. Direct democracy imaginatively attacks this alienation; the question is whether, especially in the complex, industrialized nations of the twentieth century, it is a real alternative.

SUGGESTED READINGS

(Titles are listed chronologically. All are available in paperback or other inexpensive editions.)

Plato. *Apology* and *Crito*
———. *The Republic*
Aristotle. *Politics*, Books I–IV
Epicurus. *Letters, Principal Doctrines and Vatican Sayings*
Marcus Aurelius. *Meditations*
Saint Augustine. *The Political Writings of St. Augustine.* Ed. by Henry Paolucci (Regnery). Chapters 1–3
Saint Thomas Aquinas. *The Political Writings of St. Thomas Aquinas.* Ed. by Dino Bigongiari (Hafner). Pp. 159–195.
Machiavelli, Niccolo. *The Prince*
Hobbes, Thomas. *Leviathan,* First and Second Parts
Rousseau, Jean Jacques. *The Social Contract*
Paine, Thomas. *The Rights of Man*
Mill, John Stuart. *Representative Government*
Marx, Karl. *The Civil War in France*
Green, Thomas Hill. *Lectures on the Principles of Political Obligation*
Bosanquet, Bernard. *The Philosophical Theory of the State*
Niebuhr, Reinhold. *Moral Man and Immoral Society*
Lindsay, A. D. *The Modern Democratic State*
Niebuhr, Reinhold. *The Children of Light and the Children of Darkness*
MacIver, R. M. *The Web of Government*
Tillich, Paul. *Love, Power, and Justice*
Jouvenel, Bertrand de. *Sovereignty*
Arendt, Hannah. *The Human Condition*

CHAPTER

5

Restraints on Power

Because all power is morally dubious — hard to justify and likely to corrupt — the confinement of power to its proper bounds is one of the central problems of civilization. Power constantly tends to become arbitrary and limitless. Tyranny is one of the ancient afflictions of man's collective existence. But power has never in history been so boundless and destructive as in some of the totalitarian dictatorships of the twentieth century. These regimes have made it plain that, contrary to Hobbes, not only the lack of a central power but also the lawlessness of a central power renders man's life "solitary, poor, nasty, brutish, and short." To ask about the proper limits on power and how these limits can be enforced is to inquire how life can be made decent and civilized.

Limits on power are basically of two kinds: moral and constitutional. Moral limits are those deriving from moral law, or from what is believed to be moral law; their efficacy depends solely on moral convictions. For a government to refrain from using murder as an instrument of foreign policy, even when murder is within the scope of its legal powers, would exemplify respect for a moral limit. Constitutional limits may derive ultimately from a moral law, but what makes them constitutional is their embodiment in a basic "positive" law — a law that takes precedence over all other laws and is actually upheld by society or enforced in the courts. This law may be represented by one supreme document, as in America, or it may be merely the content of a body of customs, statutes, court decisions, and historical documents, as in Great Britain. A constitutional government is one that is limited by such a law.

We shall discuss both moral and constitutional limits, beginning with moral limits because they often underlie constitutional limits. First we shall consider what may well be the oldest and most fundamental question concerning the relationship of morals and politics.

16

Are governments exempt from the moral restraints incumbent on private individuals?

One great political thinker, Machiavelli, has argued that they are, and he has become notorious for doing so. We have already taken note of Machiavelli's belief that there can be no order among men and nothing accomplished in human affairs without power. A companion belief, expressed throughout his writings, is that effective use of power is incompatible with strict observance of the moral law. No ideals can be realized without doing evil. If one is to perceive the somewhat tragic coloring of Machiavelli's argument, it is necessary to understand that Machiavelli never expressed indifference to the moral law and never glorified evil. The greatness of Machiavelli's thought depends on the tension inherent in the idea that there is a moral law but that political man on occasion must break it.

No such necessity, however, can be acquiesced in by private individuals. Rulers must sometimes be immoral in order to establish and preserve the state; for the sake of the same end, subjects must always be moral. Social order would collapse if private individuals considered themselves free to break the moral law when their interests require it. The political universe thus is morally unique.

By setting forth this point of view, Machiavelli gained one of the most unsavory reputations in the history of thought.

Shakespeare referred to him as "the murderous Machiavel," and among the synonyms of "Machiavellian" in Roget's *Thesaurus* are "false," "crafty," and "dishonest." What is most striking when one looks to the opposing arguments, however, is how faint and infrequent they are. So far as I am aware, the chief works of political thought contain no argument, answering to Machiavelli's, for the same uncompromising morality among rulers that is expected of private individuals. One great thinker who disagreed with Machiavelli was Immanuel Kant (1724–1804), but in none of his great works does he systematically take issue with the Machiavellian argument. Many thinkers have believed that the health of the political order depends on the moral rectitude of its members. Machiavelli, however, believed this too; his writings abound in expressions of admiration for the honor and probity of the ancient Romans.

Where Machiavelli differs from the others is in saying explicitly what they seldom deny: While political order depends on respect for moral standards, it depends also on the capacity of rulers occasionally to violate those standards. In view of the silence of the great political thinkers concerning an idea so unsettling as this, one wonders whether it is Machiavelli's chief distinction to have divulged a shameful truth (one writer speaks of his "appalling sincerity") that others have been too discreet to acknowledge.

Opposition to Machiavelli, then, comes less from political philosophy than from common moral convictions. But can people with these convictions hold their ground in the face of political reality? Let us consider lying as an example. Anyone who is repelled by the evasive and deceptive speech that is common in the political world should consider these two questions: (1) Could a government operate successfully if it invariably made public all of its plans and all of the information at its disposal? (2) Should a government refuse to lie even if it might thus gain some great good like ending a war or helping an underprivileged group? It is possible to answer affirmatively to both questions, but that is not the side of plausibility and common sense. Rather, these questions tend to lead one to the Machiavellian conclusion that at least so far as truthfulness is concerned we cannot really demand from rulers the same kind of morality we expect of personal associates.

But having moved this far toward Machiavelli, one should ask whether *every* moral limit is conditional on political circumstances. If one may lie to reach a political goal, may one kill? Machiavelli answered affirmatively, defending not only political deceit but also political murder. But if we go this far, then what is left of ideals and conscience? Is reality so coldly rational that profoundly evil means can effect ends that are good? The Communist regimes of Russia and China have been willing to engage in large-scale killing for the sake of community, but so far in neither place has community been attained.

This view of the matter is from the standpoint of the peculiar necessities that presumably bear on power holders but not on private citizens. The crux of Machiavelli's position is a thesis concerning these necessities: The structure of reality is such that the laws of power (that is, the rules governing its effective use) cannot possibly coincide uniformly with the laws of morality.

Another consideration entering into this question, although not conclusively deciding it, is the nature of the moral law. We may here employ the distinction made above (Question 3) between moral absolutism and moral relativism: Moral absolutism is the theory that there is a moral law, derived in most conceptions from nature or from God and independent of the interests and opinions both of individuals and societies while moral relativism is the theory that morality is relative to some variable circumstance such as the desires of the individual or the needs of society.

At first glance it may seem as though one's decision between these‘alternatives would altogether determine his answer to the question of whether governments are exempt from the moral restraints that are incumbent on private individuals. Absolutism would seem to bar all exemptions and relativism to admit exemptions without limit.

Issues in the field of political theory can seldom be conclusively settled, however, merely through a direct inference from some philosophical principle. So it is in this instance. It is possible to argue that a moral law must be broken, but that it is nevertheless in some sense absolute. For example, it may be said that "Thou shalt not kill" is an absolute law even though under certain conditions, as in war, killing is unavoidable. One may object that the word "absolute" means unconditional, and thus should not be applied to a law which must sometimes be broken. But is it not possible that certain acts that are unavoidable in some circumstances, such as lying or killing, remain evil regardless of the circumstances in which they are committed? Is it not possible that one may be in some sense guilty for doing something which circumstances made it necessary to do?

On the other side, whether relativism opens the way for an affirmative answer to the main question under consideration depends on exactly what the moral law is relative to. If it is relative to each individual's desires and circumstances, then those who possess power are not subject to the same moral restraints as those who do not; if morality is relative to the culture or the species, then both governments and governed may logically be subject to identical laws.

These remarks are intended as warnings against oversimplification, not as indications of normal patterns of thought. There is no doubt that absolutism tends to bar any distinction between the morality of politics and the morality of private life. One may escape this implication, but only by establishing two principles: Necessity bars full adherence to the moral law, and one is morally bound to pay some regard to necessity. In other words, it must be shown that perfect morality is a practical impossibility — owing not to the weaknesses of human nature but to the conditions of human life. It may be possible to do this. The point, however, is that moral absolutism affirms a single, all-embracing moral order; in this sense it does place governments under the same moral restraints that are incumbent on private individuals. Any violation of those restraints requires a particular justification if it is to be in any sense legitimate; and even such a justification may not relieve those who violate the moral law from all guilt. From this standpoint politics may be viewed as a sphere of moral tension and even of moral tragedy.

Relativism, for its part, creates the possibility of arguing that political leaders and private citizens inhabit two different moral universes or that political leaders are not within any moral universe at all. For example, if morality were held to concern only relationships among members of the same nation, then international relations would not be subject to any moral rules; political leaders would be free, in their diplomatic and military activities, to act as they please, responsible only to the moral bonds uniting them to their own subjects. Moral relativism establishes the possibility of arguing even that the possession of power entails liberation from all moral rules. In this situation political leaders would not be morally restrained even in relation to their own subjects. They would live not in their own unique moral universe but in a moral void.

There is a sense in which moral relativism clears the air. It does not subject political man to the strain of acknowledging the authority of moral rules that he is forced by circumstances to break. He can act, with clear conscience, under his own separate rules. The shadows of moral tragedy that are cast over political life by moral absolutism thus are dispelled.

This relief from tension may strike the reader as wholesome. But I suggest that there are serious risks inherent in answering affirmatively the question we are considering. These risks are particularly great when one completely abandons the idea that governments and private individuals inhabit a single moral universe. If "power tends to corrupt" under the best circumstances then surely this tendency toward corruption is enhanced where power means liberation from ordinary moral restraints. Further, if government is exempt from the moral standards applying to ordinary citizens, must government not be beyond the moral judgment of those citizens? And if government is beyond their moral judgment, is it not beyond their political judgment as well? And if this is so, is it not an irresponsible government? Of course, moral absolutism does not eliminate these risks, but it does draw attention to them.

Can one perhaps circumvent a host of moral dangers and philosophical difficulties by simply insisting on the same moral standards for everyone and refusing to grant any exceptions? Perhaps one can. In entertaining this possibility, however, one may begin to sense that it invites an idealistic distortion of reality. The political scene in the twentieth century has displayed so many paradoxes and terrors that we are bound to doubt that political realities can be dealt with as unequivocally as the moral law, in its majesty and its simplicity, may seem to demand.

Reflecting on power in relation to moral restraints leads to the matter of constitutional restraints. The difference between these two types of restraint, as pointed out above, is that one is based on moral consciousness, the other on law. Both, however, give rise to broadly similar doubts when imposed on the possessors of power; these doubts concern the wisdom of subjecting governments to invariable limits without regard to variable circumstances. Thus the question that follows will be parallel, in its general purport, to the question we have just been considering.

17

Can a government be legitimate
if it is exempt from constitutional restraints?

If we take the word "legitimate" in the narrowest sense, the answer is bound to be no, for "legitimate" in that sense merely means "lawful." A lawless government would, by definition, be illegitimate. The word must therefore be understood more broadly, as it was in Question 13 above. With this understanding, the question is whether a government that is subject to no constitutional restraints is by that fact deprived of all moral validity and of any rightful claim to our obedience.

The issue has been forcefully posed by the twentieth-century conflict between democratic and totalitarian nations. During World War II and the early stages of the Cold War it was tempting to see the democracies as the good side and the dictatorships as the bad side. But there is a growing realization that good and evil are not quite so neatly distributed and that there is not only much evil in those countries where government is restrained by constitutional limitations but that the evil may be in some measure protected by the limitations. For example, in the United States, by far the richest country that has ever existed, a number of people are hungry and undernourished. Would this be so if the government were not severely inhibited by a variety of substantive and procedural limitations laid down in the Constitution?

No political idea in the West has greater authority than constitutionalism. For over two thousand years there has been a remarkably wide and stable consensus that government ought to be carried on within a publicly known and enforceable set of restraints. Perhaps the most influential modern expression of this consensus is found in the writings of John Locke. But Locke is only one of several great thinkers of modern times who have been firmly committed constitutionalists. Locke's views in this matter, moreover, were drawn from a solidly established medieval tradition, which had in turn grown out of an ancient Greek and Roman constitutionalist tradition. Few other ideas can claim so impressive a background. Time after time, reaching back to the beginnings of thought, lawless government has been condemned as monstrous and unnatural.

The opposition to this tradition, however, is substantial — in the quality of those representing it, at least, if not in their numbers. No great thinkers have been exponents of real totalitarianism, that is, of governmental control of every detail of life, but several have been enemies of constitutionalism. Three stand out in the history of thought, and each represents a different motive.

1. Plato was opposed to constitutionalism because of his faith in the wisdom of a few. Later in life, when he faced the improbability that the wise could ever gain power, he endorsed constitutionalism. But earlier, entertaining the notion that philosophers might become kings, he opposed the subjection of government to preestablished limitations. He did this on the logical grounds that perfect wisdom is quite competent to decide for itself how far its power should reach. Plato likened the philosopher-king to a doctor, who is not hampered by prior rules but in each particular case can prescribe precisely what he deems to be appropriate.

Today we do not have Plato's faith in philosophers. But we do accept the Platonic ideal in a somewhat different form; we assume, or many of us assume, that our social problems will yield only when attacked by scientific expertise. It is scientific and technological rather than philosophical intelligence that commands our trust. Thus it may logically be asked whether we in America, with a government confined by limitations established in the eighteenth century, can bring to bear on such problems as poverty and urban disorder the full resources of twentieth-century social and physical science. The American constitution makes it next to impossible for a scientifically devised plan to be uncompromisingly applied to any of our major social problems. This problem results partly from the procedural forms for decision making that are inherent in constitutionalism and that the American constitution imposes. These forms assure that every measure finally decided upon embodies a great number of compromises; these compromises may well render the measure acceptable to the various interests affected by it, but they inevitably rob it of its scientific integrity. But beyond the procedural limitations are the subtantive limitations. Under a constitutional government, people cannot be forced to move, to alter their living habits, to take certain jobs, or to do any number of things that science might determine to be necessary for solving certain social problems.

It is not too much to say that constitutionalism and scientific government are incompatible. Which is of greater importance? This is the question Plato puts before us.

2. Hobbes was opposed to constitutionalism because of his pessimistic appraisal of man's nature. Numerous passages in Hobbes's writings show that he did not desire or even envision the possibility of anything like modern totalitarianism. Nevertheless, he regarded human beings as far too restless and selfish, too inherently chaotic, to be able to afford governments that were barred absolutely from certain areas of life. Hobbes's views on religious toleration exemplify this attitude. While Hobbes was far from being the kind of ideologue or fanatic who wants to impose a single set of beliefs on everyone, he thought it indispensable that government have the power to regulate religious creeds and forms of worship. An inviolable rule of toleration would invite a reopening of "the war of all against all."

In quiet American suburbs today Hobbes may seem a mere doctrinaire pessimist. But looking beyond the suburbs, have not the cities, with their poverty and racial tensions, become

Hobbesian worlds? And is not the whole globe Hobbesian, divided as it is among suspicious, heavily armed nations?

The impact of such conditions on constitutional government is apparent in the demand, looking to the safety of life and property, that police have latitude to deal with criminal suspects with whatever harshness and guile seem necessary for discovering and suppressing crime and that they not be bound by every rule a careful judge might find in the constitution. A very Hobbesian demand! There are probably Hobbesian sentiments also behind the apparent willingness of many people that presidents should be subject to few constitutional restraints in dealing with foreign affairs. The principles applied to both domestic crime and to international conflict are the same: Order is prior to all other values, and in some circumstances order depends on authoritarian rule.

3. If Plato opposed constitutionalism out of faith in the few, Rousseau did so out of faith in the many. Granted, such a statement has to be severely qualified. Rousseau never explicitly attacked constitutional government. Moreover, he was passionately committed to the aspect of constitutionalism calling for government through law; he held that no command of the sovereign populace could be valid unless it took the form of law. (The idea of government through law is constitutional because it implies a certain limitation on government — that it must always adhere to the form of law; it is only one aspect of constitutionalism, however, because, while adhering to the form of law, a government might regulate religion, speech, and every other individual activity.) Nevertheless, the example of Rousseau demonstrates that the idea of government by the people can take on a totalitarian flavor. Just as Plato assumed that no human agency could have the wisdom or right to restrain the most wise and righteous of all men, the philosopher-kings, so Rousseau held that no one could properly impose limitations on the people except the people themselves. In his prescriptions for organizing the state, Rousseau seems to envision a commonwealth in which the lives of individuals are absorbed into the common life and regulated in every detail by the popular will. Rousseau calls for a "civil religion," for example; this would be, as he describes it, "a

civil profession of faith of which the Sovereign should fix the articles, not exactly as religious dogmas, but as social sentiments without which a man cannot be a good citizen or a faithful subject." [1] Rousseau declares that anyone refusing to subscribe to the articles of this faith should be banished and that anyone who does subscribe to them and then "behaves as if he does not believe them" should be put to death.

Democratic totalitarianism is remote from the spirit and the structure of the American constitution, but it is not hard to see signs of it in the actions of militant students. In campus uprisings the normal proceedings of universities have been disrupted, opponents have been shouted down, and "nonnegotiable demands" have been made. Student gatherings have often been characterized by an impassioned unanimity that may have been in some sense democratic but, in its intolerance of disagreement and its lack of restraint, was far from constitutional.

Rebelling students have often asserted that the established pattern of restraints, both within universities and in the society at large, is designed to preserve the status quo, along with inequalities and injustices which it is imperative to destroy. Perhaps this is so. However, the assertion gives rise to questions of the utmost seriousness. Is constitutionalism harmful, rather than valuable, when unaccompanied by justice? Is constitutionalism a lesser value than justice? Is justice likely to be achieved through the actions of crowds so sure of their own righteousness that they refuse to abide by any rules but their own?

In asking these questions we have come upon a fourth possible reason for opposition to constitutionalism, that it stands in the way of reaching full justice. However it seems unnecessary to go any further in order to establish the point that although constitutionalism is an ancient tradition, with great moral authority, it is not invulnerable to serious doubts. It may come into conflict with ideals that have great moral authority of their own — the unrestricted application of human intelligence to social problems, order, peace, democracy, and justice.

[1] *Ibid.*, p. 139.

The list could easily be lengthened. There are values other than constitutionalism, and reality is not so conveniently arranged that these other values are, in all circumstances, fully compatible with constitutionalism. If it were otherwise, there would be far less difficulty and tension in man's historical existence — and perhaps, mysteriously, less grandeur as well.

The point at which we have arrived, then, is this: There are reasons that might induce someone to say, in answer to the question we are considering, "Yes, a government can be legitimate although it is exempt from constitutional restraints." It may be held that government is legitimized by the quality of the intelligence it represents, by its indispensability for overcoming chaos, or by its popular origins. Very simply, one is faced with the question as to how important constitutional restraints really are.

This question is so serious, not only for defending one's general political outlook but also for taking positions in relation to some of the most pressing problems of our time, that it seems worth looking at it for a moment from a completely different vantage point.

According to a widespread consensus among political thinkers, power can be confined within constitutional boundaries only by being divided. Hence, supporters of constitutionalism are invariably supporters also of divided power, while those who favor power that is wholly responsive to the judgments of those wielding it, unrestrained by prior limitations, generally favor concentrated power.

Let us then reflect on the question of whether there should be more than one main center of power in a society. From this angle, one may see things that did not become apparent during the preceding discussion.

The idea that power should be divided among two or more independent centers rests, as the reader might expect, on a tradition that is no less ancient and authoritative than that supporting the idea of constitutional government. When Plato faced the improbability that philosophers would ever gain power, he concluded that it would be wise to avoid concentrating power in any single group; instead, power should be divided between those with characteristics indicative of wisdom (such as age) and those chosen by lot, thus representing the populace as a whole. This idea, touched upon briefly in our consideration of the question, "Who should rule?" is usually referred to as the idea of "the mixed state." It was probably old, as common sense although not as political philosophy, even when Plato was writing, and it has endured both in common sense and in political philosophy to the present day. It has assumed a great many different forms, one of them the form prescribed in the American constitution. Throughout its long history and in all of its varieties, it has been rooted in one primary conviction: Totally concentrated power menaces decent and civilized existence.

Even Christian orthodoxy, which might be expected to dictate priestly sovereignty, contains its own unique version of the principle of divided power. This is the "doctrine of the two swords," which was set forth by Pope Gelasius near the end of the fifth century and has been followed in some form by almost every succeeding Christian thinker. According to this doctrine, not all power should rest in the same hands, not even in the hands of the Pope. Human beings should not be under the exclusive control of a single sword. True, most Christian thinkers, not only during the Middle Ages but well into modern times, held that there should be only a single church. However, they did not for the most part argue that this one church itself should govern or should totally control the government. The task of assuring temporal order, as distinguished from that of guiding men toward salvation, should be under a separate authority.

Protestant and atheistic critics of the Middle Ages are quick to point out that Christian thinkers of earlier times were almost never really tolerant and liberal, and that the doctrine of the two swords was often construed in a way that set the Church over the state so decisively that the spirit of the doctrine, although not its form, was denied. All of this must be admitted. Nevertheless, the tenacity of the doctrine of the two swords remains impressive. It shows that even devout Christians, certain as most of them were that God had spoken clearly and fully and had authorized a particular human organization to interpret and guard his word, shared the traditional Western mistrust of concentrated power.

American institutions, it can be seen, represent something

many times older than America itself. The separation of powers among the three branches of government is a variation on a theme that can be traced back at least as far as Plato and the Greeks. The separation of church and state is a version of the medieval principle that even authority derived from God does not justify undivided power.

Thus it seems that one can hardly avoid saying that there should be more than one main center of power in a society — at least as a general principle. Perhaps, however, there are other things of greater importance, such as achieving scientific government, order and peace, or complete democracy. It is striking that every thinker cited above as an opponent of constitutionalism was an opponent also of divided power. For Plato, philosopher-kings would not check one another, even when sharing power, for all possessed perfect understanding and therefore could not disagree; for them to be checked by men of lesser understanding, of course, would be intolerable. For Hobbes, any division of power was an invitation to chaos. And for Rousseau, the dispersal of power among separate centers was undesirable since it meant limiting the sovereignty of the people.

As pointed out in discussing the constitutional limits on power, these thinkers are not out-of-date. They represent attitudes that are powerful in the twentieth century. Plato calls for the comprehensive and organized use of knowledge in solving social problems, Hobbes for the utmost efficiency in keeping order, and Rousseau for the unchecked ascendancy of the people. All of these demands are insistently voiced in our time, and all, at least implicitly, are demands for concentrated power. Are there good grounds for resisting them?

To go much further in reflecting on constitutionalism, one subject in particular needs attention, and that is freedom. For many people on both sides the crux of the matter is freedom. In modern times, the authority of the constitutionalist and the mixed-state tradition derives primarily from the assumption that constitutionalism and divided power bring freedom, or at least that they are necessary for freedom. On the other side, much of the opposition to this tradition comes from the conviction that it does not show the way to freedom, or else that it shows the way to only a paltry freedom. Many student rebels, for example, have felt that life under the American constitution is so trivialized and debased that it is not genuinely free.

What we must consider, then, are the relations between constitutionalism and freedom.

18

Is a person who lives under a constitutional government necessarily free?

The question sounds innocuous. However, it has probably given rise to as much conflict as any question in this book. Let us, to begin with, take note of three different answers, which are basically three different definitions of freedom.

First, freedom consists simply in not being subject to arbitrary and excessive requirements on the part of the government. Thus, the answer to the question is: Yes, those who live under a constitutional government — a government barred from imposing arbitrary and excessive requirements — are necessarily free. The main prerequisite of freedom is a set of effective constitutional restraints.

Second, freedom consists in not being subject to arbitrary and excessive requirements from any source whatever — from a government, an employer, a relative, or anyone else. One might live under a constitutional government and still, for example, be continually under the despotic gaze of an employer with the power to take away one's livelihood. Would that be freedom? Only as a legal formality, surely, and not as a reality of life. Freedom depends not on constitutional government alone but on a social order so arranged that every major power, whether governmental or otherwise, is held within preestablished limitations. Thus laws forbidding racial discrimination in hiring, or in accepting hotel guests, can enlarge the freedom of individuals; a great many such laws may be needed before those living under any particular constitutional government are really free.

Third, freedom is not merely the absence of restrictions imposed by some particular outside power; it is the capacity for action. One might live under a constitutional government and in a society where every power is under preestablished restraints and still not be free. One would be unfree if he were unemployed or illiterate or psychotic; one would be unfree if he lived in a society providing few opportunities for acting constructively or creatively — in business, for example, or in the arts. Freedom, according to this view, depends on a whole set of political, social, and personal conditions.

These three concepts of freedom are also, by implication, concepts concerning governmental power. According to the first, the main demand we should place on government is that, aside from performing certain elementary functions like protecting our property, it leave us alone. According to the second concept, however, which interprets freedom as the absence of interference from any source whatever, government might (to borrow a phrase from the English political philosopher Bernard Bosanquet) "hinder hindrances" to freedom. For example, if a government prevents employers from discriminating racially, then it hinders hindrances to the freedom of minority races. The third concept, that of freedom as the capacity for action, suggests even wider uses of power for creating the conditions of freedom. A government might enlarge the areas of freedom by such means as establishing adult education programs or mental health centers.

Such apparently dry distinctions define the front lines of some of the great political battles of the twentieth century. In customary terminology, at least as employed in contemporary America, "conservatives" are those who adhere to the Lockean concept of freedom and maintain that constitutionalism alone is the principal condition of freedom. "Liberals" argue that freedom depends on government that not only is subject to constitutional restraints but that also protects individuals against nongovernmental powers. The third concept of freedom and of the role of government cannot be quite so definitely labeled, but roughly speaking it is "radical." In present circumstances it leads to the claim that freedom depends on a completely new environment. To create and protect that environment may require government of a wholly different kind from the constitutional government idealized by conservatives and liberals; creating the new environment, for example, may require highly concentrated authority, whereas later on the government might come so thoroughly under the control of a united populace that as a coercive institution it would "wither away."

These issues have arisen primarily from one of the most decisive events in man's history, the industrial revolution. In the preindustrial era it was relatively easy to assume that constitutionalism alone would assure freedom because after the disintegration of the Catholic Church during the Reformation, the government was the largest and most threatening power in existence; if the government did not endanger freedom, presumably freedom was not endangered. With the industrial revolution, however, great manufacturing and financial organizations, not altogether controlled by governments and sometimes themselves controlling governments, came into existence. It was obvious that such organizations might deprive individuals of their freedom, and they did. Many laborers in nineteenth-century England, for example, had to work more than twelve hours a day; their working conditions were likely to ruin their health while they still were young; their living spaces (it does not seem appropriate to call them "homes") were nearly always crowded and filthy; they were so badly paid that their wives and children (the children often when they were only a few years old) also had to work. Judged by "conservative" standards, such people were free; in actuality, of course, they were slaves. "Liberals" saw that this was so (defining the term "liberal" broadly enough to include many who called themselves "socialists"), and they saw also that laborers might become more free if the government, beyond adhering to constitutional restraints itself, were to enforce certain restraints on the employers.

Until fairly recently, both in England and America, the "liberals" seemed destined to vanquish the "conservatives" completely. It seemed as though a humane and well-informed person just about had to be "liberal." Today, however, the situation is not so clear. The primary reason for this is that the results of governmental efforts to "hinder hindrances" to freedom have been disappointing. Such efforts have not failed altogether, but they have not done away with conditions like poverty and racial injustice; thus they have failed for certain groups. And they have not created for anyone living conditions that seem truly liberating. The poverty and squalor of the average black person's life in America today, and the dullness and demoralization of Socialist Britain, exemplify the conditions that have brought disenchantment with liberalism.

Disenchantment, of course, is not refutation. One argument in behalf of liberalism is that it has failed only where it has not been applied. It may be said, for example, that it has not remedied racial injustice in America because conservatives have so far successfully resisted the use of governmental power on an adequate scale. Arguments of this kind can be plausible, but no longer do they seem conclusive. There is an apparent disproportion between the governmental efforts of recent decades and the advances actually made; the former seem immense, the latter meager. As a result, liberals now are on the defensive.

On one side, the old idea that freedom depends on the initiative of individuals rather than of governments and that the main condition of freedom is simply constitutionalism, has regained a certain amount of vigor. This has meant, among other things, a resurgence of conservatism. It is possible now to oppose the social welfare programs of government without appearing to be purely obstructive or reactionary.

In addition to a resurgent conservatism, a certain kind of progressivism has come into being with the revival of old-fashioned constitutionalism. The major precedents for this progressivism lie in the trade-union movement. It is based on the idea that private individuals should join together and create the conditions of their own freedom, as the unions did in bargaining for better wages and working conditions. This view seems to be present in some segments, at least, of the black-power movement. Thus when blacks organize a boycott against stores engaged in overpricing, they are working for their own liberation; they are not doing this according to traditional liberal tactics, for they are not relying on government.

On the other side, liberals are attacked by a more vociferous and self-confident radicalism than they have, at least in America, ever faced before. Distinctions here cannot be drawn with a sharpness that places every person definitely in one category and in no other. It might be difficult, for example, to know whether certain blacks should be classified under the antigovernmental progressivism discussed above or under the radicalism we are concerned with here. Nevertheless, setting aside problems of individual classification and looking at society as a whole, we find the radical attitude to be dramatically in evidence. On the one hand, it reveals a commitment to social transformation of a depth and swiftness that no government of the American type and probably no constitutional government of any kind could effect. In this respect it is authoritarian. On the other hand, it reveals a desire for a government that is far more decentralized and democratic than most constitutional regimes. One breathes here the atmosphere of totalitarian democracy that was noted in discussing Rousseau.

Let me summarily restate the issues: Does constitutionalism assure freedom? Or is it merely a prerequisite of freedom, with the realization of freedom dependent in addition on governmental action or group initiative? Or is constitutionalism actually an obstacle to freedom? It is probable that Americans will be forced to answer these questions, in one way or another, almost every day in coming years.

The idea of government under preestablished limits and the idea of government without such limits are alike unsatisfactory. The former implies that good rulers will be hindered; the latter that bad rulers will not; the former means compromise and delay in carrying out the best of plans, the latter expeditious accomplishment of the worst. It is not surprising that since the beginnings of political thought men have sought to avoid both horns of the dilemma and to discover how government might be restrained from doing evil but not from doing good. One might think of several possible solutions, such as arranging matters so that the interests of rulers and ruled are identical. One possible solution, however, stands out from the others for its simplicity and appeal. Government might be restrained from doing what it ought not to do, but not from doing what it ought to do, by being placed in the hands of persons with understanding and wisdom. In short, constitutions might be replaced by absolute philosophical knowledge, by religious revelation, or by science. Is there any validity in such a notion?

19

Can power ever be placed wholly in the service of perfect knowledge?

Flawless, all-encompassing knowledge has been the object of perennial hope. Plato powerfully expressed this hope in his ideal of the philosopher, one who had ascended from the cave of ignorance into the light of "the Good." Many Christians have believed that perfect understanding has been given to man through Christ, although man could never through reason have found his own way to that understanding. In modern times, faith in Christ has declined, but faith in reason, comparable in intensity to Plato's although based on a different concept of reason, has reawakened with the progress of science.

Can governments ever be made the servants of such knowledge? The idea that they can has naturally accompanied the hope that perfect knowledge might be attained. Plato thought that philosophers should be kings. Medieval Christians were continually tempted, in spite of the doctrine of the two swords, to grant the Pope a power as limitless and unified as they believed Christian revelation to be. The modern political imagination has long been fascinated by the idea of technocracy, government carried on by masters of technology and science.

The idea of joining power and perfect knowledge perhaps has serious flaws, but at the very least it is noble and attractive. It represents the ineradicable feeling that was noted in connection with constitutionalism: It is one of the greatest of all evils to be helplessly subject to the whims and ignorance of another human being. The idea of constitutionalism is that rulers should be compelled to stay within certain legal boundaries. The idea of subordinating government to perfect knowledge is much more radical. It proposes that the very willfulness and ignorance that necessitate legal boundaries be eliminated. Thus it envisions doing away with arbitrary government by cutting its roots in human nature. What constitutionalism would merely check — capriciousness and stupidity — perfect knowledge would wholly abolish.

The notion that this is possible, however, rests on two assumptions. The first is that perfect knowledge is available, at least to some. The second is that this knowledge has the power of determining the behavior of its possessors, transmitting to them, as it were, its own perfection. Both of these assumptions have frequently been challenged.

As for the first, one of the most widespread attitudes during the last century or two has been what might be called "epistemological discouragement," that is, discouragement over the possibility of gaining sure and comprehensive knowledge (*epistēmē*, in the Greek). In the past, especially in the Middle Ages, it was widely believed that such knowledge, comprehending man's origin, nature, and end, had been given to us by God; reason might help us in laying hold of it, but ultimately it rested on a divine guarantee. By now, however, that faith is weak if not dead. Optimistic churchmen may cite figures showing increasing church attendance, but even the churchmen themselves are more likely to study man by reading social science than by pondering the New Testament.

It is often assumed that faith has been defeated by science. That is an oversimplification. It is an ominous fact that modern man has lost faith not only in Christian revelation but in science as well. Of course everyone would agree that scientists have made striking discoveries. The question is whether there is any absolute truth contained in these discoveries. Do they concern reality itself or only our perceptions of reality?

As early as the eighteenth century David Hume (1711–1776) argued that neither observation nor reasoning can validate the universal and invariable physical laws that scientists claim to establish. Hume was one of the major sources of our "eptistemological discouragement." The most profound and influential attempt to answer Hume and to show that true and certain knowledge is possible was made by Immanual Kant

(1724–1804). Kant's *Critique of Pure Reason*, one of the greatest classics in philosophical literature, is in its immediate intent a defense of science. According to Kant, however, scientific laws derive the universal and invariable character that makes them scientific from the structure of the human mind rather than from the structure of reality itself. Reality is unknowable; indeed, it would be unwarranted to think that reality itself even has a structure. Thus Kant's defense of science is highly equivocal. It offers assurance that it is possible to frame scientific laws that are absolutely valid. But they are absolutely valid only in telling us how man *must* understand certain realities; in telling us how *man* must understand those realities and not what the realities are in themselves, the laws are purely relative.

Thus Kant too became an important source of epistemological discouragement, contrary to his own intentions. One of the most dramatic contemporary signs of Kant's influence and of the weakness of modern man's faith in science, is existentialism. Many different philosophies and attitudes have been referred to as "existentialist." If any single theme is common to them all, it is probably the idea, deriving ultimately from Kant, that man is not an object of knowledge; at least he is not that and nothing more. He is a subject — one who *has* knowledge (or perhaps does not have knowledge) and therefore is not even in principle completely knowable. One may gain understanding of humanity by looking into himself but not by objective rational analysis.

If this is so, then of course the changeless, all-inclusive knowledge envisioned by Plato and by many admirers of modern science, is not available. The ideal of government dedicated to the service of such knowledge is no better than a noble and sophisticated dream.

A number of serious and able people do not agree with such critics of reason; not everyone is totally discouraged about the possibilities of knowledge. Few would deny, however, that the critics have done much to set the mood of our time — a mood strikingly in contrast both with the confident faith of the Middle Ages and the rationalistic self-confidence of antiquity. It is hard not to wonder today whether we can know anything at all except, perhaps, that we inhabit an impenetrable darkness.

The possibility of perfect knowledge is not the only matter we have to consider. In asking whether governments can ever become servants of perfect knowledge we must also inquire whether, if such knowledge were gained, men would be disposed to respect it. They might not; they might know all things, yet behave impulsively and foolishly. One can at least conceive of mankind as having finally filled out and perfected both the physical and social sciences, yet still being stupidly and brutally governed. It is not obvious that perfect knowledge means perfect virtue.

Some thinkers have held that even though an equation of perfect knowledge and perfect virtue may not be obvious, it is nevertheless valid. Socrates apparently believed that full knowledge — that is, knowledge of man's nature and needs and knowledge of what is really good — leads inevitably to moral excellence. One who knows, fully and certainly, what is good is bound to choose it; thus an evil man must be an ignorant man. In other words, knowledge — full and profound knowledge — cannot be misused.

Socrates' identification of knowledge and virtue has been a powerful influence in history. It underlay not only Plato's concept of the philosopher-king but antiquity's long-sustained commitment to the cultivation of reason. It has probably also contributed substantially, albeit indirectly, to the good conscience and unhesitating enthusiasm with which most of us, in modern times, have supported the advance of science. We have assumed rather casually that the progress of science is bound to mean the improvement of life.

In recent decades this assumption has come to appear increasingly dubious. We have gained vast quantities of knowledge through the physical sciences and the social sciences, but we seem as likely to use this knowledge for evil ends like nuclear warfare and "brainwashing" as for good ends like peace and the elimination of poverty. It is easy to feel now that we are menaced, rather than saved, by our knowledge.

If this is so, why is it so? Is it because our knowledge is still imperfect and incomplete? Or was Socrates wrong and is it possible for individuals and peoples to be masters of knowledge and still to be selfish and cruel?

During the past century or two the most resolute defenders

of the hope that power will sometime be wholly subordinated to perfect knowledge have probably been social scientists of various kinds. This is not to say that every social scientist is a utopian, with no reservations concerning either the possible perfection or the social efficacy of the knowledge he and his colleagues are pursuing. Such reservations, nevertheless, have not been prominent in the writings of sociologists, psychologists, and political scientists. On the contrary, the effort to establish social sciences comparable in precision and certainty to the physical sciences has been pressed so aggressively that those favoring intuitive or philosophical approaches have had to fight for survival.

Few would question either that we can gain *some* scientific knowledge of society or that such knowledge would be useful in solving our problems. What is in question, rather, is whether all of our social problems are susceptible of scientific solutions and whether, therefore, all of our intellectual energies and resources should be devoted to the development of the social sciences. Is anything understood through art, philosophy, or religion that cannot be understood with greater precision and assurance through science? Might social science flourish while life in general becomes shallow and barbaric?

The Western tradition provides a weighty alternative to the Socratic viewpoint. While Socrates apparently believed that every effort of life should be centered on knowing good and evil, the Book of Genesis indicates mythically that this knowing is the very essence of iniquity. Adam and Eve were cast out of Paradise after violating God's command and tasting fruit from "the tree of the knowledge of good and evil."

The dilemma of our civilization may be symbolized in terms of these two great sources of understanding. One exalts the human mind and leads logically to the ideal of government directed and restrained by a knowledge comprehending all needs and all means to their satisfaction. The other humbles us and tells us that as long as we seek to be "as gods, knowing good and evil," we will suffer the anguish of labor, estrangement, and mortality.

Can we tell, by reflecting on this deep and apparently conflicting counsel, what has brought us to the disorder and despair of the twentieth century? Is the real meaning of Socrates's life contained in the symbol of the serpent that tempted Adam and Eve? Or has our mistake been that in following Socrates, we have somehow done so insensitively or perversely, perhaps without understanding where he really wished to lead us? Or is it conceivable that the deepest wisdom would find the counsel given by the dialogues of Socrates and the Book of Genesis to be fundamentally harmonious or even the same?

SUGGESTED READINGS

(Titles are listed chronologically. All are available in paperback or other inexpensive editions.)

Plato. *The Republic*
Cicero, Marcus Tullius. *On the Commonwealth*
Saint Thomas Aquinas. *The Political Writings of St. Thomas Aquinas.* Ed. by Dino Bigongiari. (Hafner). Pp. 175–195
Machiavelli, Niccolo. *The Discourses*
Hobbes, Thomas. *Leviathan,* Second Part
Locke, John. *The Second Treatise of Government*
Rousseau, Jean Jacques. *The Social Contract*
Hamilton, Jay, and Madison. *The Federalist*
Bosanquet, Bernard. *The Philosophical Theory of the State*
Ruggiero, Guido de. *The History of European Liberalism*
Wheare, K. C. *Modern Constitutions*
Lippman, Walter. *The Public Philosophy*

The Ends of Power

Power must be used as well as restrained. In carrying on political thinking, therefore, we must consider the ends of power. As one might surmise, this is no easy undertaking; it incorporates two large and refractory problems. First of all, what are the ends of human life in general? Clearly it is impossible to understand anything about the purpose of government without understanding something about the purpose of life in general. But this has been an enigma for every generation. Some of the thinkers of our own day — Jean-Paul Sartre is perhaps the greatest of these — have reached the seemingly despairing conclusion that human life has no purpose whatever. But once we have identified the ends of life, then we must estimate what power can do in helping us to reach them. Power cannot do everything; it cannot, for example, make one person love another. What can it do?

Thus thought concerning the ends of power can go astray in two ways — by misconstruing the ends of life and by misunderstanding the capacities of power.

The difficulty of thinking about the ends of power, however, is matched by the importance of doing so, especially now, when there is deep confusion concerning the proper activities of men and governments. Our confusion probably has several sources; such conditions as the ceaseless, planless rearranging of our lives by technology and the permeation of thought and feeling by the fads cultivated by commercialized television may disorient us far more deeply than we realize. Whatever the causes of our confusion, the political consequences are not likely to be negligible. Lacking wise and settled purposes, we devote our resources and attention to secondary problems — exploring space, for example, rather than eliminating poverty. And we will be immensely fortunate if we do nothing worse than concentrate on secondary problems. The time may come, for example, when we will be sorely tempted to escape the burden of discord and uncertainty by placing absolute power in the hands of some leader or party claiming superhuman insight. In one way or another, if we sink unprotestingly into a state of doubt and indifference regarding the ends of power, those ends are likely to be set by irresponsible and insensitive men who feel themselves unchecked by the moral and political consciousness of other men.

For these reasons, reflecting on the ends of power is not a leisured diversion but an urgent and practical duty. But in so difficult a task, where should we begin?

A person's first thought, in asking what government should do, is likely to be that whatever the value pursued it should be one that all can share. The good at which power aims should be a common good. This is apt to seem elementary. But is it? Is there any such thing as a value that all can share? And do not those who have power always pursue their own good in preference to others, even when their intentions are idealistic? Let us then ask at the outset whether every government does not necessarily pursue the good of only a portion of the society, that portion controlling the government.

20

Does every government serve merely "the interest of the stronger"?

The phrase, "the interest of the stronger," and the argument that it describes the goal of every government are attributed in *The Republic* to an actual contemporary of Socrates, a philosopher and teacher named Thrasymachus. In effect, Thrasymachus held that men are estranged in essence; hence it is meaningless to speak of "the common good" or "the general welfare." The ends of each man are solely his own and not those of anyone else, and they are likely to be in conflict with the ends of others. Everyone with power, consequently, seeks his own good alone and sacrifices the welfare of others to attain it. It follows that every social and political order, even the most ancient and venerated, and even the most carefully designed, is fraudulent. Societies have usually claimed the sanction of both God and the people; they are fraudulent because what they actually do, and are intended to do, according to Thrasymachus, is to further "the interest of the stronger," that is, of those in and behind the government.

Probably no great thinker has wholly agreed with Thrasymachus. Some thinkers, though, have been so deeply suspicious of established governments that they have assumed that most do, in fact, serve only "the interest of the stronger," even though there might be some exceptional condition, like philosophers becoming kings, that would enable them to do otherwise. An example of this attitude is Karl Marx.

Marx, of course, believed that the working class was destined finally to seize all power for itself. With this event, government would come so completely and obviously to serve the interest of all that it would no longer even have to exercise coercion; the state would "wither away." Until that time, however, governments must inevitably betray the interests of most of the people. Marx saw the liberal democracies of his time as little better than disguised dictatorships carried on in the interests of the upper classes. Such devices as written constitutions, representative assemblies, and popular elections, which supposedly compelled governments to serve the interests of their subjects, were instruments of fraud; they were seen as elaborate devices for veiling the tyranny of landowners, industrialists, and financiers.

Marx's view stemmed partly from his conviction that the decisive power in any society was in the hands of those owning the means of production. Less decisive were the various governmental instruments of power, such as the police. In certain circumstances governments might gain independence from class control, but the tendency was for them to be instruments of the dominant economic class. Thus governments were simply in no position to serve the common good. But perhaps a more crucial point, for Marx, was that in a society divided among warring classes there could be no common good; the interest of one class he saw as necessarily the oppression or destruction of another class. Even a philosopher-king could not devise a formula that would bring together the bourgeoisie and the proletariat.

These were the considerations which placed Marx provisionally on the side of Thrasymachus. Marx qualified Thrasymachus's position by adding, "until the Communist revolution"; otherwise, he wholly agreed that the "justice" maintained by governments is nothing but the "interest of the stronger."

It would hardly be too much to say that refuting Thrasymachus has been the principal aim of political thought. Plato devoted the whole of *The Republic* to this task. Of course, not all thinkers have had Thrasymachus consciously in mind, but most of them have tried to show that government can further some state of affairs that is not merely in the interest of the stronger but is in the interest of all. Even so cynical a thinker as Hobbes argued emphatically that peace is needed by everyone; men like Rousseau and Marx, who thought that governments rarely if ever sought a common good, concentrated on showing how the reign of selfishness might be overcome. When recent liberalism, in response to Marxist criticism, tried to show that liberal and democratic regimes could act in the interest of workers as well as of owners, they were simply renewing the ancient effort to refute Thrasymachus.

Can this be done? One's answer will probably depend on whether he believes that in essence people are estranged or united. In even a just society some members must get less — of leisure, job satisfaction, wealth, and so forth — than they would like to have. This is strikingly true of soldiers who lose their lives in battle, of workers who perform indispensable but stultifying jobs, and of criminals who are caught. The problem is to show that such people are not, in every conceivable case, merely the weak who are sacrificed in the interest of the strong.

This can be done, thus refuting Thrasymachus, only if all are so essentially united that society can be organized so that those who sacrifice conscious desires for the good of others actually make those sacrifices for a truly common good and thus for their own highest good, and are not merely means to the ends of others.

At first glance, such an idea may seem far-fetched. But in actuality it is not as distant from common sense as it may seem to be. We do not generally think of a soldier who has lost his life in war (unless, perhaps, in an unjust war) as someone weak who has been victimized by the strong. Nor do we ordinarily think in this way of a criminal who is spending time in prison. The fate of each is felt to be in some way justified. How? By serving some end, such as the survival of the nation or the maintenance of justice, which is assumed to be more important to each person even than his life. This not to say that people always feel this way, but probably they usually do; otherwise the governments over them would depend purely on force in order to survive.

But instead of getting involved in such complicated questions, can we not simply say that each one has his own interests that here and there coincide with those of others, thus making society possible? In this way we would avoid speaking of such mysterious things as a "highest good" that is also a "common good," and that may be completely unknown to the one whose good it is. The trouble is — and this is the reason why we cannot resort to so attractively simple an expedient as this — that the *conscious* interests of millions of people rarely, if ever, do coincide. Not even such elemental values as order and peace are desired by absolutely everyone; revolutions and wars always provide examples of people who profit from chaos. Social order therefore necessarily depends on some coercion; usually this takes the form of peaceful pressure, although no society can avoid the occasional use of open force. But this coercion must simply be an assertion of the "interest of the stronger" unless it is exercised in behalf of some ultimate common good. Such a good must be the good of those coerced, if it is truly common, but must also be unperceived by those people or else they would not have to be coerced. In short, since people cannot be at one in their *conscious* interests, they must be at one in their *real* or *highest* interests. Otherwise, every government serves merely "the interest of the stronger."

The issue of moral absolutism versus moral relativism is closely linked with this question. If there are absolute moral laws or absolute values, then these must in some way define a common good; otherwise they would not be both good and absolute. Thus, for example, a moral absolutist might regard justice as a good to which every purely individual interest is properly subordinate; the imprisonment suffered by a criminal would be something demanded by his own essential nature.

On the other hand, if all moral rules and all values are relative to circumstances or persons — if they merely represent someone's idea of what is good and not good in itself — then it is questionable whether the idea of a truly common good makes any sense. It may be that a moral relativist is logically bound to side with Thrasymachus; certainly Plato's attack on Thrasymachus was an attack on moral relativism in general. However, the paths of thought are intricate enough to make the assertion of an invariable rule in this matter inadvisable. Many relativists have been no less hostile toward the outlook represented by Thrasymachus than was Plato.

In speculating on this question, we are traversing what is probably the most rugged and uninviting terrain in the whole realm of political theory. But there is no way of passing around it. A political system is essentially a set of arrangements by which some people dominate others. How can this be made morally tolerable? All civilized life is carried on under a great moral shadow. More explicitly, all civilized life must be assumed to rest on exploitation of the weak, unless we can show that Thrasymachus was wrong and that it is possible in the nature of things for government to be carried on in the interest of all.

At this point let us assume that the present question has been answered negatively, establishing by implication the principle that governments can and should serve the common good. What is this good?

Out of the din of modern history, there is one answer that comes clearly to our ears. That is liberty. The cry of liberty is heard, perhaps more compellingly than any other, in the French and American revolutions; liberty is the central value in liberalism, the rise of which can be traced back to the Renaissance and which has dominated European and American political life for almost two centuries. This is not a unanimous answer, as is shown by Communism, which accords equality and community priority over liberty. But Communism has been a conscious revolt against a liberal tradition that has admittedly been dominant. The same is true of other antiliberal movements, such as conservatism and Fascism; their rebellious temper testifies to the ascendancy of the liberalism they reject.

It seems appropriate, therefore, that we should reflect on the ends of government by reflecting on liberty.

21

Is the ultimate purpose of government simply to guarantee liberty?

Among the ideological hurricanes sweeping through our century, one is bound to wish that he could discover, as a refuge from confusion, the true ultimate purpose of government. Here we are asked whether we can do this simply by falling back on the tradition in which most of us have been raised.

The idea of liberty, for all of its nobility and its apparent simplicity, is probably as difficult to handle as any idea in the field of political theory. This is partly because it is very easy to slip into identifying liberty with some other value. Here is how this happens. Liberty is presumably doing what you want to do. But that is ambiguous. Does it mean doing what you happen to want to do at the moment or what in the long run will bring you satisfaction? Does liberty consist in following your immediate desires or in following the demands of your real nature?

So far, the reader may feel that no very difficult problem has arisen. A thoughtful and conscientious person is likely to reject the idea that you are really free in doing what you feel like doing if what ensues is merely frustration and misery; liberty, then, is following the demands of your real nature rather than mere momentary impulses. The sequence of thoughts may seem reasonable enough up to this point. Actually, it is here the trouble begins, for next one must ask what the demands of man's real nature are. Various answers are possible; some have said justice, some community, some happiness, some another value. But whatever the answer, at this point liberty has turned into something else. One is free when he is just, or living in a community, or happy. There may well be some substance to such ideas. The only trouble is that in talking about them, one is no longer talking about liberty as a distinctive value.

Another reason why the idea of liberty is hard to deal with is that it can be plausibly argued that liberty is a condition of every other value — that justice, community, and so forth depend for their value on being freely chosen. This may well be correct, but it is a confusing idea. It is confusing, for it can seem to imply, because liberty must be chosen along with whatever other value is chosen, that liberty is an end in itself. What it really implies, though, is only that liberty is a kind of universal means.

In reflecting on the present question, then, one may find it helpful to stick to a purely negative concept of liberty, that is, to think of liberty simply as a state of not being interfered with. According to this view, a person is free when he is in a position to do what he wants to do, regardless of whether doing it is going to meet the demands of his real nature and bring satisfaction or not. This may strike one as an impoverished concept of liberty, but any other is apt to land one in a philosophical morass.

In addition, one may find it helpful to assume that the only way of answering the question before us affirmatively is by saying that liberty — *so far as government is concerned* — is an end in itself. To say, for example, that the ultimate purpose of government is to promote community, but that community in its nature has to be freely chosen and therefore governments must always promote liberty, is not to say, "Yes," in answer to the question. "Yes" can be said only by asserting that the ultimate purpose of government is to put man in that unhindered state that is liberty.

Having established these two premises, how can we proceed? I suggest that an appropriate step is to try to "get the lay of the land" by noting some of the major alternative definitions of the ultimate purpose of government. The following four should suffice for this purpose, although some readers may think of others to add on their own.

1. *Equality.* This is the ultimate purpose of government as defined by many proponents of democracy, socialism, and communism. Often equality is paired with liberty, and the two values together are treated as the ultimate purpose of government. It is doubtful, however, that equality and liberty are altogether compatible. Is it not likely, for example, that complete equalization in the sphere of economics would require many infringements on liberty?

2. *Civilization.* This alternative is embraced by those who hold that a government's primary task is to protect the infinitely complex set of customs, traditions, and institutions that is inherited (except possibly by societies engaged in revolution) from past generations. Because such an inherited order is likely to incorporate both inequalities and restraints, it is difficult to accept civilization as the end of government and still to put a very high value on equality or liberty. If equality is the characteristic value of democrats, socialists, and communists, civilization is the end sought by those who are often called conservatives.

3. *Happiness.* Nowadays it is often assumed that gaining happiness is the purpose behind every other purpose, and that no value, such as equality or civilization, can be defended except on the grounds that it leads to happiness. This assumption can be valid only if one defines happiness so broadly that every possible sense of satisfaction or achievement is seen as an example of happiness; in that case the proposition that man's ultimate aim is happiness is nothing more than a truism. Thus with happiness, as with liberty, one must be careful not to equate it with every other value. Dostoevsky offers us an example of the kind of distinction one must be able to make. Dostoevsky held that freedom causes unhappiness; "nothing has ever been more insupportable for a man and a human society," he asserted, "than freedom." [1] At the same time, however, he placed freedom among man's ultimate values.

[1] Fyodor Dostoevsky, *The Brothers Karamazov,* translated by Constance Garnett (New York: The Modern Library, n.d.), p. 262.

4. *Justice.* This has often been taken by philosophers to be the highest political value; it is the central theme, for example, of Plato's *Republic.* Again one must be wary of blurring the lines between values. It may be, for example, that securely establishing justice would require placing drastic limitations on liberty; it is conceivable that perfect justice, however noble and compelling an ideal it may be, would not make many people happy.

Answering the question of whether the ultimate purpose of government is simply to guarantee liberty now becomes a matter of choosing among alternatives. Is the true end of government liberty, or is it equality, civilization, happiness, or justice? Or is it some other value, one we have not considered?

The problem a reader faces is that of making a choice, even a tentative choice, that is reasoned and not arbitrary. This problem brings us back to the theme emphasized in the introduction: Most or all political positions are grounded in some particular concept of man. This theme applies in a very clear fashion to the question before us. How one conceives of the purpose of government depends on how he conceives of man. Hobbes once remarked that "whosoever looketh into himself . . . shall thereby read and know . . . all other men." [2] Hence, to choose among the alternatives before us, one must look into himself and try to "read all other men." Let us see what kinds of readings support the above alternatives.

1. Equality is apt to be the end affirmed by those who are struck by some great likeness among men — a characteristic that seems to overshadow in importance all other human characteristics and that seems to be shared by every being who can be called human. Conscience has been regarded by some thinkers as a supremely important and universal trait of this kind. On a very elemental level, the finitude and mortality that are common to all of us might be viewed as equalizing characteristics.

2. The aspect of human nature that typically preoccupies conservatives is the extent to which that nature is formed by society. If a human being is deprived of all of the characteris-

[2] Hobbes, *op. cit.*, p. 6.

tics he derives from society, he is no longer, except in his potentialities, human; he is a peculiar kind of beast. From this it may be inferred that the ultimate purpose of government is that of preserving civilization; this is the task of preserving humanity itself.

3. Is there anything distinctively human that is lost when all is subordinated to happiness — freedom, for example? John Stuart Mill expressed the idea that something is lost, in his famous statement that "it is better to be a human being dissatisfied than a pig satisfied; better to be Socrates dissatisfied than a fool satisfied." [3] The idea that happiness is the true end of government perhaps rests on a certain humility, an abstinence from proclaiming resounding ideals and an unwillingness to ascribe to man any trait that exalts him above living nature. Perhaps it rests as well on a certain pity for men in all the incalculable misery they have endured.

4. The idea that justice is the ultimate end of government is closely associated with the view that the essence of man is reason and that the major function of reason is to enable man to participate in the order of being. Justice is right order. Perhaps the only view of man that implies a total denial of the value of justice is that expressed by Thrasymachus, namely, that there is no principle higher than that of egotism. But anyone who believes that passion or faith contributes more to human life than does reason, or who sees creativity, for example, as a higher value than order, would be inclined to assign justice a subordinate place in the hierarchy of values.

What vision of man will lead one to reject all of these possibilities and to hold that the ultimate purpose of government is guaranteeing liberty?

Liberalism has often been characterized by its critics as no more than a rationalization of the interests of one class, the bourgeoisie. Thus the subtitle of one well-known book on liberalism is *The Philosophy of a Business Civilization.*[4] This

---

[3] John Stuart Mill, *Utilitarianism, Liberty, and Representative Government,* introduction by A. D. Lindsay (New York: E. P. Dutton and Co., 1951), p. 12.

[4] Harold Laski, *The Rise of European Liberalism: The Philosophy of a Business Civilization* (New York: Harper, 1936).

subtitle says, by implication, that the ideal of liberty (assuming that liberalism rests on this ideal) is not based on any respectably profound interpretation of the nature of man at all.

No one nowadays, in view of all that has been learned from Marx about the role of classes, would deny that the major force supporting liberty in the modern world has been the bourgeoisie. But this does not mean that liberty is no more than the value of a single class. A universal value, after all, may be promoted for selfish reasons; if this were not so, indeed, universal values would have gained very little recognition.

If liberalism is construed as a universal philosophy and not merely a class philosophy, what is the view of man underlying it? First of all, it would seem, some kind of individualism, that is, a view in which likenesses or connections among individuals are emphasized less than the distinct and unique being of each individual himself. The liberal must be someone affected above all by the glory of the separate self.

In addition, to be a liberal, one probably must believe in the reasonableness of that separate self. Liberals almost always have, and this seems to be because if men were not reasonable, liberty would not be practicable. Such a conclusion seems especially applicable to the twentieth century, when many of our problems, such as those of crime and environmental destruction, bespeak a collective unreasonableness and suggest the need for centralized and unlimited power.

Perhaps we are living in the twilight of the liberal era; the tendency of politically conscious students to embrace either radicalism or conservatism is one sign of this. And if we are, perhaps it is just as well; such values as equality and civilization are not obviously inferior in dignity to liberty. Nevertheless, we should not watch the passing of liberalism complacently, as though it would entail no dangers; nor should we watch it thoughtlessly, without asking whether mankind is really prepared to put something better in its place. For while it is possible that there are better things than liberty, twentieth-century history makes it clear beyond any question that there are worse.

Having considered the ultimate ends of power, let us now consider the more proximate ends. A list of possible questions in this area would be endless. There is one question, however, a very broad one having to do with economics, that has had an important role in the political debates of recent times and seems fitted for giving us access to wide regions of political thought.

22

Should the government own the major means of production?

This question is wider in scope than may at first be apparent. It is not concerned merely with industries. The phrase "means of production" refers to land, mines, water power, communications, and so forth, as well as to factories. Nor is it concerned with production only, apart from distribution. It is only to avoid redundancy that distribution is not explicitly mentioned; it may be assumed that whoever controls production controls distribution as well.

What is asked about in effect is man's responsibility for the earth — for the whole material setting of human life and for all of the materials that can be used for the maintenance and improvement of life.

An old idea, accepted by both Locke and Marx, the fathers respectively of "free enterprise" and of socialism, is that the earth is the common possession of mankind. By some primal right, established by God or inhering in the nature of things, it belongs to all. But how can mankind actually take the earth into its possession and use it — by allowing individuals freely to appropriate parts of it, or by placing it in the custody of governments?

The answer, endorsed in one way or another by all defenders of capitalism, was given by Locke when he asserted that "the Condition of Humane life, which requires Labour and Materials to work on, necessarily introduces *private Possessions.*"[5] While the earth *belongs* to mankind, it can be *used* only by individuals; and for individuals effectively to use things, they must own them. Hence the government's responsibility for the earth is fulfilled in protecting the rights of property. Thus ran Locke's argument.

[5] Locke, *op. cit.*, p. 310. The italics are Locke's.

Is it true, however, that efficient use of the earth requires individual appropriation? Does not the history of industrialism indicate, on the contrary, that our exploitation of the earth depends on immense economic organizations and that the individual alone can do almost nothing? Locke asserts that one has a right to keep "the Acorns he picks up under an Oak, or the Apples he gathered from the Trees in the Wood." [6] What relevance have such examples to the industrial systems of the twentieth century? Today in America hardly a single item of daily use is the product of individual labor. Our cars, clothing, food, household utensils, and so forth, all come out of large, intricate productive organizations, and these organizations in turn are integrated into vast national economic systems.

Furthermore, does not the history of capitalism indicate that free appropriation by some entails complete deprivation for many others? It has been urged, of course, that those who are able to appropriate a great deal vindicate by this very ability their right to all they appropriate, while those who have nothing thus prove that they deserve nothing. One may well be suspicious, however, of a logic that begins with the principle of man's common ownership of the earth and ends with the principle that a few can rightfully take most of it for themselves. It is not surprising that this logic has not been universally accepted.

It has also been urged, of course, that individual appropriation is not only just, whatever the inequalities that result, but also that it is beneficial for everyone. The few who gain great wealth for themselves also, it is said, create great wealth for society. America, with its vast concentrations of private wealth along with the historically unparalleled prosperity enjoyed by the majority, is evidence in favor of this argument. But it is not conclusive evidence. Given America's natural advantages, an economic system other than capitalism might have produced goods just as abundantly while distributing them more equitably. Further, as has often been noted in recent years, while great numbers in America are prosperous, a sizable minority is not. In view of the ugliness and squalor of the inner cities, America's poor today may be more wretched than

[6] *Ibid.*, p. 306.

the poor in most other societies either of the present or of the past.

It is understandable, then, that a number of thinkers have sought alternatives to individual appropriation. Such thinkers usually are called socialists.

Socialism in the broadest sense represents the simple idea that mankind must assert its primal right to the earth by actually taking the earth into its possession and using it co-operatively. Socialists have not agreed whether this should be done through governmental action or in some other way. There are several kinds of socialism. What unites them all, however, is unwillingness to tolerate private appropriation of the earth.

Socialism has drawn much of its moral force from the democratic tradition. According to this tradition government should be carried on only with the consent, if not the active involvement, of the governed. Power belongs to the people. But property, of course, is power; thus extensive concentrations of private property within a democratic society at least are anomalous. It has seemed to most socialists that democracy and capitalism are flatly contradictory. This judgment comes out in some of Marx's bitter comments, in *Capital*, on the despotic organization of factories. Thus socialism has often been conceived by its proponents as an extension to the economic sphere of democratic principles already widely accepted within the political sphere.

A contrary opinion, of course, often is heard in America. Here democracy in politics and capitalism in economics often are treated as natural allies.

One of the most serious questions with respect to socialism is whether *common* appropriation can, in practice, mean anything but *governmental* appropriation. Most socialists would refuse to assent to any such equation. Socialist literature is filled with ideas for voluntary cooperation. Many socialists are scarcely more trustful of government than are typical capitalists, and Communists of course go so far as to anticipate "the withering away of the state."

In practice, however, common appropriation has nearly always meant governmental appropriation; and Communism, as everyone knows, has led to something very different from "the withering away of the state." Do we see here signs of an insuperable difficulty in the whole socialist idea? Perhaps if all of us together are to appropriate the earth, this must be done through the one agency that represents all of us together, namely, the government. An economic enterprise might, of course, be taken over by a cooperative group smaller than the whole society; a factory, for example, might be run by the workers. But this is not the same as common ownership; and it may be argued that a worker-run factory is not more likely to behave responsibly in relation to society as a whole than is a capitalist-run factory. It may be, then, that government is a socialist's only recourse.

The trouble is that government ownership and common ownership are not at all the same. It never occurs to Americans, for example, to think of the postal service, with all of its buildings and equipment, as their common property; it belongs to the government and they are fully aware that that is a different matter altogether. This is not to suggest that governmental ownership is necessarily a bad thing. It might in some circumstances contribute both to efficiency and to public responsibility. But such advantages cannot be taken for granted; even if they are realized, governmental direction of the economy, with the powerful officialdom and pervasive bureaucratic procedures that inevitably go with it, is far from the ideal of common appropriation that is the foundation of socialism.

There is one way, indeed, in which governmental control of the economy may be even further from common ownership than is a regime of private ownership. Governmental control unites the political and economic centers of power. Thus, these do not check one another, as they occasionally do within a capitalist system. This would not matter if the government were held fully responsible to the people. But governmental responsibility is apt to be very imperfectly realized even in the most democratic of countries; and as government becomes larger and more complex, popular understanding and control may grow weaker. In this way socialism could mean, directly contrary to its original intent, that power is more concentrated and uncontrolled than it would be under a system of private ownership.

In this kind of impasse the common sense of the typical American immediately suggests that the truth is somewhere between the two extremes. And indeed such a suggestion is not without weight. In the history of political thought it is probably Thomas Aquinas (1225?–1274?) who has most clearly delineated a theory that sanctions neither unrestrained individual appropriation nor total governmental control. Aquinas argued that property should be held by individuals but that it should be regulated by law and custom to assure its being used in the common interest. He maintained, as an American businessman might, that a person would more carefully look after what is his own than what is held in common, and that the economy would, therefore, be better managed under a system of private property than under any other system. At the same time, Aquinas condemned the use of property primarily for personal profit; it should be used for the common good, and society has a right to see that it is. On this side of his thought, Aquinas seems less like an American businessman than like the socialist whom the businessman would excoriate as a dangerous radical.

Is the issue thus resolved? No one should quickly conclude that it is. In actual political practice, it may often be sagacious to profess a middle position; in political thinking, however, it is often only a way of avoiding issues. Thus, one must ask whether the Thomist position resolves the dilemma of private versus governmental ownership or whether it merely obscures it. There is room for doubt.

Does the right of individual ownership, according to the middle position, mean that an individual can, if he insists, appropriate and use some significant part of the earth according to his own desires and contrary to the will of society? If it does mean this, then what is ostensibly an intermediate position turns out to be, in essence, an individualism like that made explicit by Locke. If it does not mean this, however, and the individual's use of his property can be supervised and controlled by society, then one might question how significant the right of individual ownership actually is. In substance, the theory would seem to be one of common ownership. If, finally, it is sometimes the individual and sometimes society that is responsible for the earth, then it must be explained where the line between the two is to be drawn and how disputes between them are to be decided; otherwise, what is offered is less a theory of property than it is an argument to the effect that property questions are not appropriately subject to prior theoretical determination. The latter may, of course, be the truth.

The question of whether individuals should be free to appropriate the earth has always been important, but it has never been as important as it is today, because technology has placed the earth much more fully at man's disposal than it has ever been before. The right of individual appropriation is a much more sweeping power than it was in the days of Locke. Private persons have used the earth in ways that have decisively affected whole nations. The lives of the American people, for example, have probably been shaped as significantly in the twentieth century by General Motors as by the Supreme Court. Is it right, then, that General Motors be private property? On the other hand, if one has any mistrust of government, then the immensity of the powers entailed in the ownership of certain kinds of property may be the very fact that makes one unwilling to resort to governmental appropriation.

Is there any way, having developed the power to work spectacular and devastating effects on the earth, of fulfilling the spirit of the biblical assertion that "the heaven, even the heavens, are the Lord's: but the earth hath he given to the children of men"? [7]

In discussing the present question, we have been concerned primarily with the physical aspect of life. However, "man shall not live by bread alone," and while twentieth-century America has been preoccupied with material goals, other societies and other ages have been concerned mainly with goals of the spirit, such as faith, morality, and beauty. The time may come when Americans are ready to reconsider their relationship to such goals. Many have gained material plenty and have found it not only insufficient but even stultifying and demoralizing.

The following question is designed to explore this aspect of governmental responsibility.

[7] Psalm 115:16.

23

Does government have any important spiritual functions?

Today one is likely to be surprised that the question is even asked. The same person who is convinced that government has responsibility for the material welfare of individuals is apt to be equally sure that it has no responsibility whatever for their spiritual welfare. Has the matter not been definitively settled through the principle of separation between state and church? The individualism that was once axiomatic in economic matters has now become axiomatic in spiritual matters.

This is perhaps a very good thing. It seems worth noting, however, that some of the greatest thinkers have not been of the same mind as most present-day Americans; they have not shared either our spiritual individualism or our political secularism.

Moreover, aside from what has been thought in the past, is it not on the face of it doubtful that so fundamental a question should be absolutely and permanently closed? Perhaps not, if "spiritual" be taken to refer only to what falls within the purview of the churches. But this is far too restrictive a definition. In Webster's Dictionary "spiritual" is defined in terms as broad as "incorporeal" and "intellectual."

For purposes of this discussion we may employ the ancient triad of values, the true, the good, and the beautiful, and say that man is spiritual insofar as he seeks those values. Given this definition, then, does government have any important spiritual functions?

Let us begin with the first of the above values, truth. Does government have any responsibility for truth, or, to bring the question nearer to the point, for the beliefs of those whom it governs? The idea that government should be wholly detached in matters of belief, and the individual left completely on his own, developed fairly recently, only two or three hundred years ago. Locke defended such a doctrine near the end of the seventeenth century. He was not the first to do so, but he spoke for an idea that was still controversial and generally unacceptable.

Moreover, the reasons earlier thinkers advanced for asserting some governmental responsibility for beliefs were not absurd. They may have been inadequate, but they were not incomprehensible or manifestly unreasonable. To begin with, these men thought that we can know with assurance what the truth is. The question, "Who is to say?" asked by many students today would have been attributed, by most of the great Greek and medieval thinkers, to laziness, confusion, or something else that blinded them to the importance and availability of objective truth about man and the universe.

Why not let each individual on his own, however, discover the truth for himself? Most of these thinkers would have made the sensible (although possibly erroneous) response that discovery of the truth is difficult even for the greatest minds and that it is altogether beyond the capacity of average minds. Consequently, if government and society give no help to the individual in deciding what to believe, the result for most people will be complete uncertainty and, finally, despair. The result for society, since social order depends on some beliefs being held firmly and in common, will be weakness and disorder.

Most thinkers of the past would not have inferred from these considerations that the government should have an exclusive and unchecked right to proclaim the truth. Nor would they have inferred that the government should try to uphold the truth with violence and terror. Aristotle, for example, held that scientists and philosophers independent of the government had primary responsibility for finding the truth and making it known, and the typical medieval thinker believed that supervision of belief was a duty pertaining first of all to the spiritual sword rather than to the temporal. Even Plato and Augustine, who were thinkers of a more radical and impassioned temper than many others, were far from desiring to see truth promoted by force. Education was the way taught by Plato; and Augustine finally sanctioned the use of violence against heretics only after long hesitation and with utmost reluctance.

But none of these thinkers, and few others until recent times, came near the modern idea that government is spiritually neutral. To know the truth was for them one of man's principal aims, and government was far too great an influence in human life to be barred from participating and helping in the common pursuit of this aim.

It is noteworthy that Locke based his individualism, in economic and spiritual matters alike, on the same broad principles and that the typical American liberal has rejected these principles in regard to property but clings to them in regard to belief. Thus, to begin with, Locke assumed a certain essential estrangement among human beings. This meant, economically, that the use one person makes of his property is not the business of anyone else; it meant, spiritually, that the beliefs of one person are of no proper concern to anyone else. In the second place, Locke assumed that despite the prevalence of estrangement (which does not necessarily eventuate in conflict) there is a natural harmony among individuals. Thus, he thought, if each one acquires and uses property according to the dictates of his own interests, order and prosperity will naturally ensue; likewise, in the spiritual realm, if each one is left free to seek out and affirm his own personal truth, universal truth will emerge spontaneously. Finally, Locke conceived of freedom primarily as absence of governmental restraint. One is economically free, therefore, if he is not being interfered with in acquiring and using property even though, as a matter of fact, he may have so little property that he is starving; at least such a view can easily be derived from Locke's theory of property. Correspondingly, Locke apparently saw a person as spiritually free so long as his beliefs were of his own choosing even if those beliefs were false and in some way spiritually destructive.

The typical liberal of the present day has left Locke far behind so far as economic theory is concerned. In considering economic questions, a contemporary liberal is likely to assume (1) that human beings are not essentially estranged, but that each has some responsibility for the welfare of all others; (2) that there is no natural harmony, that unrestrained accumulation of profits by individuals is, therefore, not harmless but leads to drastic inequalities and to cycles of inflation and depression, and that a just and stable economic order consequently depends on governmental action; and (3) that freedom to starve is not real freedom.

With respect to personal belief, however, the same liberal

is likely to remain an unreconstructed follower of Locke. Is there an underlying logic holding together his seemingly divided consciousness? It is not clear that there is.

In order to test his views on this question, it might help the reader to imagine that a belief he detests — for example, that white men constitute a superior race or that America should be organized and governed by the military — has won the allegiance of a large and powerful group in the country. Would he object if the government took steps to assure that this belief was not taught in the public schools or proclaimed without opposition in the nation's press?

Let us turn to another dimension of man's spiritual life, morality. During antiquity, people were less concerned than we-are today with material welfare and less preoccupied than most people were during the Middle Ages with faith. They gave much attention, however, to morality — not as a puritanical discipline denying worldly pleasure for the sake of life beyond death but as a discipline for living fully within this world. Correspondingly, they viewed government as occupying a position of moral leadership.

Thus were the spiritual and the political fused. Is this appropriate? Does government have any responsibility for the moral character of individuals?

For most people today the answer would be, as in relation to the question of whether government has any responsibility for the beliefs of those it governs, an emphatic negative. To begin with, at least so it is commonly held, moral theories are very open to doubt. Anyone who presumes to say what is good and what is evil is putting forward a mere personal opinion, something that he cannot prove and thus should not try to force upon others. The notion that governments should define the good life and impose it on people is particularly outrageous, for governments are not wiser than private individuals; on the contrary, they are often uniquely uncomprehending. If morality is the capacity for living well, then one person has as good a claim to being moral as another. Each one has his own ideas as to what it means to live well, and each one should be allowed to hold and to practice these ideas. Besides, even if it were right for the government to try to make men moral, how could it? A moral action is one that is freely done, whereas all the government can do is to coerce. An act done under governmental pressure could not possibly be moral.

These statements represent familiar attitudes in twentieth-century America. However unthinkingly such statements may sometimes be delivered, they are not baseless or arbitrary. One can discern underneath them some of the major principles of modern liberalism, such as individualism, moral relativism, and the idea that government belongs on the periphery of life and not at its center.

However, the other side of the argument — the notion that government does have some responsibility for the moral character of individuals — is represented by thinkers of the stature of Aristotle and Thomas Aquinas and thus is not as unsound as many Americans would suppose. The argument in Aristotle might be reduced to something like the following chain of principles: Living well is not doing just as one pleases but depends on understanding and adhering to a pattern of life that, in a general way, is valid for all human beings; discovery of this pattern requires unusual insight as well as the gradual development of tradition; most people, therefore, need society to provide moral illumination and structure for their lives; government is the principal agent of society and thus is properly involved in the fulfillment of society's moral responsibilities.

This argument would not justify a government's deciding all by itself what is moral and then forcing it on people. Political power should serve a moral consciousness that is the mind and tradition of a whole culture and not something created by a government. Moreover, the moral responsibilities of government should be carried out less through coercion than through example, through education, and through the respect, rather than fear, inspired by the laws.

These two views concerning the moral functions of government (we may call them the "liberal" and the "moralistic" views) involve two very different conceptions of law and its place in life. In the liberal view, the principal purpose of law is protection; the law should assure security for persons and property and provide the individual with a sphere in which he can live as he pleases. In the moralistic view, on the other hand, the law should prescribe what is right, not merely what serves the convenience of individuals; the primary purpose of law is to help give moral form to man's life. In accordance with this basic difference, the liberal must feel that on the whole the less law there is, the better. The moralist, without being totalitarian, does not feel it undesirable that the individual should in many aspects of his life find the law at hand as a guide and monitor.

It is easy for most Americans to see the weaknesses in the moralistic view. It accords government a dangerous eminence and evinces relatively little respect for the freedom and uniqueness of personal life. The weaknesses of the liberal view, however, are not so obvious to most of us; thus it seems particularly important to point them out.

For one thing, liberals will be found often to rely on the notion that moral rules are purely subjective and personal; this is why they believe governments should not lend their weight to such rules. But are not at least some rules incumbent on everyone? Presumably those against murder and theft are; and if we admit even that much, we have given up the casual relativism so often expressed (but perhaps not so often really believed) by liberals and have acknowledged that every human life should be carried on within a moral structure that is the same for all. Some, of course, go so far as to claim that there must be rules against murder and theft only for the protection of possible victims and not because murder and theft are intrinsically wrong; thus it is said that there should be no law against self-murder, that is, suicide (which, for some reason, is always assumed to hurt no one except the person committing the act). Here one must probe as carefully and deeply as possible into his own feelings to determine whether he genuinely does look upon murder and theft as morally neutral; if one is candid with himself, he may find a more tenacious moral consciousness in himself than he had been willing to acknowledge. But even if one sticks to the claim that he cares nothing about universal morality but only about harm to others, has he saved the day for himself? Why should he care about harm to others if he is indifferent to morality? He may reply that all he really cares about is harm to himself, but that in order to protect himself he must agree to social arrangements under which everyone is protected. This is one form of the social-contract position. Perhaps there is no argument that can forcibly dislodge one who consistently adheres to this position. But such a person has committed himself to a grim and lonely redoubt.

Another weakness in the liberal view is that it places a burden of moral discernment on the average individual that may well be too heavy for him to bear. During the last generation or two we have come to realize that the *material* well-being of an individual is decisively affected by conditions prevailing in the whole society and manageable, if at all, only by the whole society; thus in time of severe unemployment an ordinary laborer is likely to suffer severely regardless of his personal initiative and ability. But is not the *moral* well-being of an individual also decisively affected by society? An individual's ideas of right and wrong are, by and large, learned from the society in which he lives. Surely it is inevitable, then, that individuals living in societies that are morally degraded or empty will suffer literally from demoralization, that is, from the confusion and apathy that must be experienced when one is unable to see that any one course of action or way of living is preferable to any other.

Finally, it may be asked of the liberal whether it is possible, even if it were desirable, to place government on the periphery of moral life. Through such influences as personal example, education, and law, it would seem as though a government must inevitably have a powerful effect on the moral attitudes and practices of citizens. If so, would it not be well for political leaders, rather than trying in vain to separate themselves from the realm of morality, to acknowledge the influence they inevitably have on morality and to exercise that influence as wisely as they can?

I suggested above that one test his principles by asking how he would feel about governmental efforts to cultivate beliefs which he deems true and wholesome. Here one may try to imagine how he would feel if the government were trying to create moral attitudes which he considers valid and desirable.

Let me address this suggestion in particular to defenders of the liberal view, because they are likely to be vastly in the majority among readers of this book. How would they feel if the government over them were taking steps through public education, through laws, and through the urging and example of leaders to cultivate in citizens tolerance for views they disagree with, acceptance of all races as equal, and concern for social and economic justice? Would this be objectionable?

As for governmental responsibility in relation to the third value, beauty, perhaps a brief comment will suffice. It would be possible to argue the affirmative side — that government does have a responsibility for beauty — from history: In two periods that are widely regarded as the most creative in Western history, the Periclean Age in ancient Greece and the era of the Italian Renaissance, governments took a direct and extensive responsibility for supporting the arts and for creating beauty in public places. This side of the matter may be more effectively argued, however, in relation to the present.

One of the most disquieting experiences of our time has been witnessing the deterioration of the environment. In part this deterioration consists in increasing filthiness, particularly of water and air. In great part, however, it consists in increasing ugliness — in the loss of natural beauty (through billboards, industrial wastes, housing developments, shopping centers, and so forth) and in the failure to create urban beauty. Virtually everyone acknowledges the government's responsibility for the environment. This is tacitly to recognize the government's responsibility for beauty.

Present-day political attitudes owe much to a self-consciously hardheaded utilitarianism that saw little relationship between politics and beauty. The objects of government, for earlier representatives of this attitude, were personal freedom and security of property. But even the reformers and radicals who appeared somewhat later were often affected by this utilitarianism; their aims were usually nothing so ethereal as beauty, but were rather dollars-and-cents values like higher wages and free medical care. What we are experiencing now, in the oppressive unsightliness of our cities and in the gradual disappearance of pristine nature, is the inadequacy of this utilitarianism. In actuality, it was quite unrealistic. Now, if one is genuinely hardheaded, he must admit that governmental neglect of beauty is neglect of one of the elementary requirements of decent and civilized existence.

This realization brings us to a vantage point from which we can look back over the whole question we have been considering. We find in connection with beauty that an element of necessity enters the picture: Government can hardly decline all responsibility for it. But does not this element enter into every phase of the question?

On one side, certain conditions forcibly demand public intervention. These include, as examples, educational needs that cannot be met by private schools and the growing squalor of the cities; some would say that the irresponsible use of television networks for private profit is among these conditions. All impose spiritual responsibilities on governmental institutions.

On the other side, governmental leaders are inevitably at the center of public attention and thus, although some of them might scoff at the whole idea of having any "spiritual functions," influence the beliefs and the moral attitudes of the people. Having spiritual *effects*, they can hardly refuse spiritual *functions*. In this way, having begun with the question of whether government *ought* to assume any spiritual functions, we have been led to the point of wondering whether it can help it.

It will by now be apparent to the reader that the traditional wall between church and state does not come near to resolving the issue before us. The relationship of the temporal and spiritual realms, assumed by many to be a problem that we have left far behind, appears after all to be among the perennial questions. It is in order to establish this, that I have presented arguments primarily on one side of the issue.

We should not forget the other side, however. Although we have found the question of a government's spiritual functions to be far more open than most people today suppose, it would be reckless casually to grant the government a primary spiritual role. The arguments separating the spiritual and the temporal, however commonplace and uninteresting they may appear as a result of endless repetition and frequent over-simplification, are very weighty. Power relationships are inherently base, for they mean that some people are at the disposal of others; owing to their inherent baseness, moreover, which tends to inspire pride in those who have power and irresponsibility in those who are subject to power, these relationships are exceedingly corruptible, tending to become morally even worse than their nature requires. Politics is the darkest area of man's collective and historical existence; that is why an ancient wisdom tells us to beware of mixing the political and the spiritual. The moral precariousness of political leadership can only be increased by spiritual responsibilities and the consequent possibility of spiritual pretensions; on the other hand, true spiritual nobility would probably seldom remain unimpaired if subjected to the necessities and temptations of political power. These dangers have been underscored by the monstrous "spiritual" polities of our time, such as Hitler's Germany and Stalin's Russia.

Having opened up this question, so seldom seriously discussed in our day, we are in a good position for considering a closely related question. One spiritual function that everyone grants the government (although a few would say that it is not a spiritual function) is that of defining and somehow dealing with crime. Let us consider in a very general way how this function should be fulfilled; we may conveniently do this by examining our views of punishment.

24

As a response to crime, is retribution inhumane?

In our time, crime is probably more often thought of as evidence of sickness than of sin. In fact, even to speak of sin, in discussing social problems, is sure to cause raised eyebrows. A student of social problems is usually not expected to accept the kind of moral absolutism that renders the word "sin" appropriate; and often he is not expected to regard the law as having to do with morality as distinguished from mere social convenience.

The sickness evident in crime is often seen, moreover, as a

sickness of the society rather than of the criminal. Crime is traced back to social conditions, such as broken families and lack of employment opportunities. When this is done, the criminal comes to be seen as a victim and society in a sense as the criminal.

It cannot be denied that there is some truth in this way of looking at crime. If the criminal were not a victim, at least in some measure, how could one explain such a well-known fact as the higher crime rates in slums as compared with suburbs? Indeed, if there were not some statistical correlation between crime rates and either social conditions or psychological conditions, that is, the sickness of either society or of the individual, then crime would be a thoroughly irrational phenomenon, entirely outside the sphere of rational explanation.

The question as to whether crime can be regarded as *altogether* in the nature of illness rather than moral transgression, however, cannot be decided by statistics. And this question is of utmost importance in that one's answer to it involves his whole conception of the nature of the individual and of the relations between individual and society.

The first issue on which one has to make up his mind is whether or not to regard the individual as wholly comprehensible through causal explanations. That is, can an individual be completely understood in terms of various laws — physical, psychological, and social — or does he in some sense stand above the various causal sequences? In other words, is man free? The view that the individual is entirely explicable in terms of causes may be termed "naturalism," for the individual is regarded as belonging altogether to the order of nature. Let us call the counterview "voluntarism," because it maintains the possibility of free or voluntary acts.

It will be apparent to the reader that naturalism is the basis of the view that crime is sickness. Presumably sickness is not freely chosen but is caused.

Where does retribution come into the matter? For naturalism, clearly, it does not come into the matter at all. If man is viewed naturalistically and crime regarded as illness rather than sin, retribution is senseless. A physician would not punish a patient for contracting pneumonia.

From a naturalistic viewpoint, two problems are present in

crime. These are the reformation of the criminal and the prevention of future crime; the first is connected primarily with the welfare of the person who committed the crime, the second with the welfare of society. Both present problems of control or management rather than of morality. The criminal must be reshaped so that he is no longer a criminal, and society must be reorganized so that it is no longer productive of crime.

One serious question concerning the naturalistic approach to crime is whether it is possible to control either the criminal or society in a way that will assure desirable results. Certainly it cannot be done as yet. Perhaps a more serious question, however, is whether the naturalistic approach, in however subtle and benign a fashion it may be, is degrading to human beings. Does it make them into things subject to manipulation by psychiatrists and social planners and thus lacking in some quality essential to their humanity? In short, does the "dignity of the individual" disappear?

Voluntarism obviously offers very different perspectives. Assuming the reality of a moral law, the principle of retribution inevitably takes on a certain amount of authority. For one thing, retribution can be seen as a way of vindicating the moral law. A crime is implicitly an attack on that law (for the sake of simplifying and abbreviating the discussion, we pass by the complicating issues that arise when legality and morality do not correspond). Retributive punishment — "eye for eye, tooth for tooth, hand for hand, foot for foot, burning for burning, wound for wound" [8] — is a counterassertion of the moral law. It is thus a restoration of true order.

For another thing, from a voluntaristic and moralistic viewpoint one can think of a criminal as deserving punishment in the sense of having a right to be punished. This idea sounds very strange. Yet if man derives his dignity from being, unlike animals, subject to a moral law, then he suffers an indignity when he is treated as being exempt from that law — which is apparently what happens if his breaking of the law does not call forth from others its counterassertion. In other words, man

[8] Exodus 21:24–25.

is treated with disrespect if he is allowed to break the law without being punished. Thus Hegel declared that an individual "does not receive . . . due honour . . . if he is treated either as a harmful animal who has to be made harmless, or with a view to deterring or reforming him." [9]

The principle of retribution, then, does not threaten the dignity of the individual, as the naturalistic approach to crime seemed to do. It is, nevertheless, surrounded by difficulties, some arising from the side of nature and some from the side of morality. The difficulties arising from the side of nature result from the unquestionable fact that man is at least in part a natural being and thus that crime — at least in part — is an illness. Thus, even assuming that the arguments in favor of retribution are valid, it cannot be denied that crime is in some measure subject to being treated and cured. In some cases retribution and therapy can be readily combined, but there is no reason to think that they always can be. For example, retributive standards might call for a long prison sentence, which would almost certainly complete and confirm the moral decay of the criminal; therapeutic standards might call for a period of hospitalization that would not be particularly punitive. The principle of retribution provides no way out of the dilemma.

A similar difficulty, rooted ultimately in man's natural being, arises from the standpoint of the interest of society. Here the dilemma is presented by the fact that the prevention of crime is imperative, yet this is not necessarily accomplished through retribution. For example, crimes might best be prevented by executing everyone who commits any crime whatever; by the standard of retribution, this would be grossly unjust. It is as impossible to ignore the problem of prevention as it is that of individual therapy; but the principle of retribution provides no way of approaching these problems.

Even from the side of morality, however, retribution does not receive unqualified support. For one thing, it seems in violation of the standard of humility. Does not one who presumes to judge the gravity of a crime lay claim to insight of a kind

---

[9] Georg Wilhelm Friedrich Hegel, *Philosophy of Right*, translated by T. M. Knox (Oxford: Clarendon Press, 1952), p. 71.

that no human being possesses — insight both into the depths of human nature and into the requirements of the moral law? Jesus said, "Judge not," and one of his reasons for saying this may have been that in judging one engages in self-deification.

An equally serious check on the principle of retribution comes from the principle of forgiveness. It is widely felt, owing largely to the influence of Christianity (although Christianity is not alone among religions in calling for forgiveness), that man stands on a higher moral plane when he is merciful than when he is punitive. To exercise mercy is presumably to withhold punishment. Some theologians have asserted the contrary, but it is hard to see it as just that a criminal might receive a punishment fitting his crime yet remain guilty with forgiveness still necessary for "clearing the books"; on the other hand, it is hard to see what forgiveness can mean unless it is an alternative way of annulling the crime, one in which the penalty is either suspended or lightened.

Some people have seen Christian humility and forgiveness as the heights of man's moral consciousness. If that is so, then it would seem that the principle of retribution is seriously challenged indeed. But humility and forgiveness are both very difficult to understand and to practice. Humility requires self-depreciation, and this for most people is highly unpleasant if not impossible; forgiveness expresses a willingness to pass over legitimate grievances and is beyond the capacity of most of us. And even if one can, why should he, engage in self-depreciation or refrain from repaying those who have injured him? Does not such conduct suggest weakness rather than virtue? Thus it must be asked whether humility and forgiveness really do mark the heights of moral consciousness.

Even if they do, however, this question remains: Are they *political* virtues? How could one gain and hold political power while abasing himself through the practice of humility? And how could a state possibly maintain order if, instead of punishing criminals, it forgave them?

On the other hand, does not the greatness of Abraham Lincoln seem to lie precisely in his humble and merciful temper?

We have now reflected rather extensively on the uses of

power — on its ultimate purposes, on its economic and spiritual functions, and on its proper response to crime. We may appropriately bring this set of reflections to a close by asking how great a role, in general, government should have in human life.

25

Should governments try to create societies that fulfill all needs and desires?

This question brings us to a position overlooking one of the great chasms in the Western political mind. On one side lies what can be called "the politics of redemption." Some of the greatest thinkers in history — Plato, Rousseau, Marx — represent this general outlook. The principle defining it is simply that the goal of politics and of political thought is a life on earth that is altogether good. There are no unconquerable evils in man or in the essential structure of earthly life. Felicity is not a gift of God, and it is not reserved for a heavenly existence or a time after death. It can be attained through human planning and it can be attained here on earth.

Exponents of this view are not generally bland optimists; they have often expressed deep hatred of the social and political world about them. But their mood has not been the resigned disenchantment of those who take it for granted that worldly happiness is unstable and unsatisfying. Their mood has been rather the impatience and disgust of those who feel that men have betrayed their potentialities. Finding themselves in hell, they have called for the creation of heaven. The communist vision of human brotherhood, arising from the conquest of all poverty, injustice, and enmity, exemplifies the politics of redemption.

On the other side of the chasm lies what I shall call "the politics of convenience." This may be based either on skepticism concerning the capacities of man and the possibilities of life on earth, as in many Christian thinkers, or, paradoxically, on satisfaction with things as they are. Both attitudes prompt a politics of low expectations and low demands, since the world either cannot or need not be much improved. Government is not called upon to bring salvation but only to enhance the convenience of life.

Thus Locke, exemplifying the politics of convenience as based on satisfaction with things as they are, did not assert that life without government would be terrible or impossible. He would not have dreamt of saying, as Rousseau did, that when man founds a government and enters into the civil state, "his faculties are so stimulated and developed, his ideas so extended, his feelings so ennobled, and his whole soul so uplifted, that, did not the abuses of this new condition often degrade him below that which he left, he would be bound to bless continually the happy moment which took him from it for ever, and, instead of a stupid and unimaginative animal, made him an intelligent being and a man." [10] That is the voice of redemptive politics. For Locke, a government may save time and annoyance by doing for men certain things that they otherwise would have to, and could, do for themselves. But that is all; it cannot turn hell into heaven.

It is a chasm, not a mere line, dividing these two concepts of power because each is normally accompanied by certain allied concepts and attitudes; each, therefore, tends to be the center point of a whole political philosophy. Thus, to begin with, those who speak for the politics of redemption are often preoccupied with the state of man's soul — for example, with his relationship to the true and the good (Plato) or his moral perfection (Rousseau); those who speak for the politics of convenience are apt to be concerned primarily with external arrangements and with their efficient and orderly control.

Again, on one side all attention is given to the public realm — logically, since there can be redemption through politics only if private life is completely subordinate to public life. On the other side, what is of greatest concern is the security of the private realm, with the public world seen primarily as a threat. Further, those thinkers who are engrossed in the state of the soul and the possibility of its renewal through reformation of the public world generally view the earth as the pos-

[10] Rousseau, *op. cit.*, pp. 18–19.

session of all men in common and wish either to regulate severely or to abolish private property; Plato, Rousseau, and Marx were all, in differing ways and degrees, enemies of private property. On the other hand, those thinkers who are concerned mainly with external arrangements and with protection of private life are apt to be, like Locke, strong defenders of personal property.

Finally, the politics of redemption is likely to be a politics of concentrated and unlimited power. Admittedly, this is not true of Marx, for whom the final redemptive act in history, the Communist Revolution, was to prepare for the disappearance of the state. But the man who first put Marxism into practice, Lenin, was an exponent of unconstitutional and highly centralized power, and both Plato and Rousseau were more or less opposed to dividing power and subjecting it to prior limitations. On the other hand, the politics of convenience is typically embodied in ideals such as constitutionalism and the mixed state. This can be easily understood. To divide power, and draw constitutional bounds around it, is obviously prudent (unless one shares Hobbes's view of man) when one's aim is merely to eliminate some of the inconveniences of daily existence and to assure the safety of life and property. It is prudent, but it is no way to bring about "new heavens and a new earth"; if that is the aim, there must be a new political order as well.

In drawing this dichotomy, I do not mean to imply that everyone must be on one side or the other. It would be hard, for example, to know where to place Hobbes; and some readers may, in developing their own political ideas, discover ways of combining redemption and convenience — or, perhaps, of choosing neither one. What I wish to suggest is simply that we encounter here a profound and dangerous issue for modern man.

Most Americans today are probably satisfied with the politics of convenience, which, with our vast resources and space, has served the greater part of the population fairly well. But there are strong and embittered minorities, such as the blacks, whom it has served quite poorly. It could be argued, of course, that this is merely because it has not been pushed far enough;

it has not been used to seek the convenience of everyone. It may be, however, that concentration on convenience so limits political imagination that minorities suffer; an orientation toward the manifest needs of majorities may be a tendency inherent in the politics of convenience.

In addition, a critic might see in this outlook another weakness that is equally serious. It is more than doubtful that convenience, even very great convenience, enjoyed equally by all classes and races would long satisfy human beings. The "sensible" man would say that political redemption is a pipe dream and that we should be satisfied if we can merely enhance the ease and comfort of life. Most people are not sensible, however, at least not in the long run. Nor is it obvious that they should be. From the time of Isaiah to that of Marx, men have imagined a time when "the eyes of the blind shall be opened and the ears of the deaf shall be unstopped," when "the parched ground shall become a pool and the thirsty land springs of water." [11] Will we be nobler and better when we cease to have such thoughts? Yet into how much terror and disappointment will they lead us?

SUGGESTED READINGS

(Titles are listed chronologically. All are available in paperback or other inexpensive editions.)

Plato. *The Republic*
Aristotle. *Nicomachean Ethics*
Saint Augustine. *The Political Writings of St. Augustine.* Ed. by Henry Paolucci (Regnery).
Saint Thomas Aquinas. *The Political Writings of St. Thomas Aquinas.* Ed. by Dino Bigongiari (Hafner). Pp. 92–158.
Locke, John. *A Letter Concerning Toleration*
———. *The Second Treatise of Government*
Mill, John Stuart. *On Liberty*
———. *Utilitarianism*
Dostoevsky, Fyodor. *Crime and Punishment*

[11] Isaiah 35:5 and 7.

Green, Thomas Hill. *Lectures on the Principles of Political Obligation*

Dickinson, G. Lowes. *A Modern Symposium*

Troeltsch, Ernst. *The Social Teaching of the Christian Churches,* 2 vols.

Buber, Martin. *Paths in Utopia*

Berdyaev, Nicholas. *The Destiny of Man*

Lippman, Walter. *The Good Society*

Schumpeter, Joseph. *Capitalism, Socialism, and Democracy*

Lindsay, A. D. *The Modern Democratic State*

Niebuhr, H. Richard. *Christ and Culture*

Galbraith, John Kenneth. *The Affluent Society*

Arendt, Hannah. *The Human Condition*

Berlin, Isaiah. *Four Essays on Liberty*

Historical Change

A leading historian of ideas has observed that "to ask earnestly the question of the ultimate meaning of history takes one's breath away; it transports us into' a vacuum which only hope and faith can fill." [1] Anyone who tries to think philosophically about history realizes immediately that this observation is true, and, moreover, that it applies not only to questions concerning the ultimate meaning of history but also to many other questions concerning history — the extent to which man can control it, the means that effective control requires, and the significance and natural tendencies of historical change. All philosophical questions, simply because they arise only as inquiry is pushed to its ultimate limits, can give one the feeling of being on the edge of a precipice; philosophical questions having to do with history seem particularly abysmal. How can we possibly speak with any assurance about the nature and course of the whole stream of human events?

It seems that we certainly cannot. Yet anyone who reflects on politics with seriousness and persistence is led inevitably to try. This is owing in large part, I think, simply to the imperfection and failure that attend all political undertakings.

[1] Karl Löwith, *Meaning in History* (Chicago: University of Chicago Press, 1949), p. 4.

Even relatively modest undertakings, like Woodrow Wilson's effort to link the United States with a global association of nations, are often blocked. Exalted ideals like those ascendant in France in 1789 and in Russia in 1917 usually lead to violence and tyranny. Are all great political ideals and efforts then futile? If not, which ones may bear fruit and under what conditions? If so, is there anything enduring, is there any place of refuge from historical change? Questions like these force themselves on the attention even of those who would prefer to ignore them.

It is not political failure alone, however, that gives rise to the philosophy of history. Even when the prospects of immediate success are good, one may find himself unexpectedly faced with an insidious little question, "What then?" Just as the present will give way to the immediate future, so that in turn will give way to the distant future. If world peace and perfect justice are achieved, what then? The answer is that the person who asks the question and all of his contemporaries will die. Any paradise that they create will be left to strange generations. Finally, too, any such paradise will itself decay and disappear. Ultimately the very earth will become uninhabitable. Many people ignore these certainties, but there is no way in which, with philosophical good conscience, we can deny them or suppress the sense of ultimate pointlessness that arises from them. It is this sense of ultimate pointlessness that prompts some of the most breathtaking questions concerning history.

Here we shall restrict ourselves to some of the more manageable queries. Let us begin with one that is rather immediate in this era of revolutionary hope and deep disappointment, a query concerning the extent to which man is in control of history.

In past ages man was inclined to assume that he was in subjection to cosmic cycles or to God. In recent centuries, however, he has come to feel that he dominates the cosmos through scientific knowledge and technology, and he has come to doubt the reality of God. His self-confidence, at least until recently, has grown immensely. He has come to think of history as a work of his own design. For Isaiah and Augustine, history was a drama written and staged by God; in recent times it has been widely thought that man himself is the author and director of this drama.

Man's most extreme claim to historical control is that voiced by certain revolutionaries: A complete and predetermined transformation of society is within the scope of human powers. Both the French and the Soviet revolutions involved such a claim. We may therefore conveniently reflect on the extent of man's historical sovereignty by asking whether man in his revolutionary self-confidence simply affirms his own proper ascendancy or whether he thus overreaches himself.

26

**Is man capable of carrying out,
and keeping under control, a total revolution?**

Certain contemporaries, from heights of idealism or from depths of bitterness, have come near, at least, to saying that he can. Student radicals in recent times, for example, seem to have believed that society might be swiftly remade through a fierce and insistent revolutionary will. Black radicals as well, although often in tones more suggestive of defiance or even of despair, occasionally have approached this extreme of revolutionary self-assurance.

These are not merely ephemeral emotions, provoked by troubled times. On the contrary, they are rooted in the self-assurance of modern man — a confidence in human power and virtue that broke forth in the Renaissance, was dramatically expressed in the French Revolution, and was apparently vindicated by the triumphs of science and industrial technology. Rousseau may serve as a good example of this attitude even though, owing more it would seem to his own peculiar temperament than to his philosophy, he had qualms about actual revolutionary undertakings.

Rousseau's savage denunciations of eighteenth-century civilization and his eloquent descriptions of the new society he envisioned would have little point apart from the assumption that regeneration is possible. Man is free to turn from decadence to renewal and in this way radically to alter the course of history. As we noted in discussing the concept of original sin, Rousseau emphatically repudiated the Augustinian idea that man has lost his original innocence. Rousseau conceded that man had become tragically entangled in historical circumstances, such as inequitable systems of property ownership, and that these had distorted his conscience and his will. Man could extricate himself, however, were he determined to do so. Rousseau began the first chapter of *The Social Contract* with the famous words, "Man is born free, and everywhere he is in chains." The book as a whole is an effort to show how those chains can be broken.

Where can a will of the requisite strength and purity be found? According to a view common in all ages, it can be found only in the most exceptional individuals, in great men and heroes. In ancient times, Alexander the Great was the object of a veritable cult; in our own times, among radicals at least, Lenin has been regarded with similar veneration. Rousseau was not free of this attitude. He was too much under the influence of ancient writers not to dream of a Lycurgus or a Solon (these were the lawgivers of Sparta and Athens respectively) who would grasp the helm of history and restore man to his original moral integrity. The general thrust of Rousseau's thought, however, is toward the idea that conscience and will in their primal innocence are to be found among the people. Great men may be needed at moments of crisis, but steady guidance of the state should come from the common men who make it up.

Claims to historical sovereignty may be based on knowledge, rather than will. For example, science, rather than the uncorrupted will of heroes or of peoples, may be counted on to give us mastery of affairs. An idea of this sort is at least in the back of the minds of many social scientists today, and among the great thinkers it was explicitly argued by John Stuart Mill (1806–1873).

In a book that is not read very much today but was widely studied in the Victorian age, *A System of Logic,* Mill expressed confidence that an authentic and all-inclusive science of society could be established. Government would then be based on empirically tested knowledge rather than on political guesswork. Mill did not think that such a science would make it possible to predict and control every detail in history; but he did think that it could provide reliable guidance for those in a position to take unpredictable details into account. The general ideal he sketched was that of history made comprehensible and controllable through science.

The idea that we can will, or scientifically plan, a new historical era reflects the hopeful, man-centered attitude of the modern world. This idea has helped to inspire not only the revolutions that have punctuated European history since 1789 but also the intense activity that has peopled and industrialized the North American continent.

In view of the present power of this idea, it is somewhat surprising to note in the Western mind an old and deep-seated tendency in the opposite direction — toward the idea that the course of history is determined by something other than the will or knowledge of man. Ancient thought, despite its intense concern with man and its confidence in the potential sweep and power of his knowledge, was conspicuously lacking in the historical self-assurance that is frequently displayed in modern thought. The sense of a fate that spells uncertainty for all plans and mortality for all societies was strong. Plato believed that even the government of philosophers was doomed finally to decay. As for Christianity, the orthodox concept of history was one of divine determinism. The life, death, and resurrection of Jesus was seen as the enactment and disclosure of God's historical intent. Man might respond or fail to respond, but he could not alter the effect of God's decisions.

Do such attitudes represent human weakness — a lack of courage or a diffidence perhaps natural to man before he had begun to discover his own scientific and industrial prowess? On the contrary: There are sound reasons for having misgivings about modern man's revolutionary self-confidence.

Some of these are epistemological, which is to say that that they have to do with the knowability of society. What they come to is this: It is highly doubtful that society can be comprehended with the kind of precision and fullness that characterizes our knowledge of physical objects. It is not only that society is highly complex. Man is part of society, and there is no apparent way in which he can stand wholly outside of it, studying it without prejudice or passion, as he might study a mineral. Even if he could, moreover, society is made up of beings who apparently are capable of choosing freely, that is, of choosing in ways that cannot be foreseen and thus cannot be incorporated in any body of knowledge; behaviorists assert that it only seems so and is not really so, but many highly competent social thinkers disagree with them on this.

If, for these reasons or others, society is in some part outside the scope of exact and certain knowledge, then man is hardly in a position to transform it at will. He cannot foresee all the consequences of his actions and thus must often produce unintended results. It has often been pointed out that both the French revolutionaries of 1789 and the Russian revolutionaries of 1917, rather than bringing about complete transformations, in large measure reestablished the old societies. For example, in its centralization, its pathologically suspicious authoritarianism, its use of secret police, and its insistence on spiritual as well as political conformity on the part of citizens, Stalinist Russia was not unlike Czarist Russia. Such unconscious repetition of the past seemingly testifies to man's historical ignorance; if he could understand his past, he would not repeat it.

Other reasons for questioning the modern revolutionary *élan* concern the qualities of human character. Belief in the possibility of total and successful revolution presupposes a very considerable confidence in man. A revolution can hardly succeed unless its authors are very good people — good enough not only to envision accurately and to pursue the good of mankind but good enough also not to be corrupted by the use of violence in which they are sure to become involved. Nor can a revolution succeed unless the populace as a whole is capable of becoming, or of being made, good; otherwise the new society is a house of cards.

It is hardly necessary to underscore the observation that there is room for doubt as to whether human nature in fact corresponds with these inescapable presuppositions. If it does not, if there are serious moral weaknesses both on the part of the revolutionary leaders and among the people at large, then a revolutionary situation invites excesses of terror and violence, and the new order, even if better than the old, is bound to provide new opportunities for misbehavior.

Thus the negative case is strong, so strong in fact that one may wonder whether it is possible even within narrow limits to set and achieve historical goals. Is it possible, for example, even to maintain stability against the forces of technological change? A great American essayist has remarked that "what actually happens when the steam engine or the dynamo or, for that matter, the automobile, the airplane, and the radio, is invented is simply this: Our hearts lift up and we let out a glad cry, 'Hold on to your hats boys, here we go again.'" [2] Is even moderation historically possible?

Whatever the answer may be, the revolutionary attitude is not likely to fade away. And strangely enough, even one who feels that there is good sense in the antirevolutionary arguments just brought forward may find himself with a lingering and inexplicable sympathy for the revolutionary side. As with the arguments for direct democracy and for the politics of redemption, they may seem to flout common sense and still to express something which should continue to be expressed.

One thing often expressed in revolutionary writing, and without which civilization might be far poorer, is a sense of the possible splendor of humanity. People who are politically moderate are apt to accept it as an ultimate and inalterable fact that human beings are mediocre and life prosaic. The ideal of human glory, which the Greeks expressed by depicting their gods as immortal and powerful human beings and which was present among Christians even more strikingly in the faith that God had been incarnate in man, is lost. The potentialities of life come to be identified with some of its most uninspiring actualities. Revolutionaries refuse to acquiesce in any such identification; they reassert the possibility of splendor.

In doing this, furthermore, not only do they bring forward a truth about man; they also, using a traditional Christian

[2] Joseph Wood Krutch, *Human Nature and the Human Condition* (New York: Random House, 1959), p. 144.

phrase, bring society "under judgment." The existing order is not allowed to represent the total possible scope of life. Even one who is dubious of revolution may hold that it is crucial to man's spiritual self-preservation to maintain the critical perspective on society that revolutionary writings often provide.

Many also will feel that there is some kind of truth in the revolutionary exaltation of man as the lord of history. This goes further than mere glorification of life: It asserts that man himself can bring the potential glory of life into full reality. In the Bible man has "dominion over the fish of the sea, and over the fowl of the air, and over every living thing that moveth upon the earth." [3] In the books of revolutionaries he has dominion over himself and his history as well. It may be said that such is an invitation to chaos and violence. That may very well be true. But assuming it is true involves certain problems — problems that may not be insoluble but are certainly serious. Is the glory of life then purely imaginary and something that can never be realized? And if man is not lord of history, what meaning can history have?

No small part of the demoralization of the present time arises from the fact that we do not know what to think about these matters. Since the beginning of World War I in 1914, a series of profound and unforeseen disasters has shaken our confidence. After a half century that has included two prolonged and ruinous wars of global proportions, a protracted economic depression, and the tyrannies of Hitler and Stalin with their calculated and extravagant violations of human dignity, we doubt that history is under the direction either of man or of any other beneficent force. Such discouragement might be fairly easily borne by a religious civilization, for faith in things beyond history would remain. But modern men have counted far less on rising above history than on dominating it, and less on entering another world than on perfecting the one we now inhabit. In these circumstances, to lose confidence in the future is to suffer a basic spiritual disorientation.

Modern man's whole view of himself and of reality thus is

[3] Genesis 1:28.

at stake in the question we are considering. The revolutionary outlook, although explicitly maintained by only a minority, is expressive of a humanistic self-confidence that has been shared by the vast majority. For modern man to become convinced that his own nature and the world's nature are such that he does not possess the capacity for revolution is not a small matter; it poses a threat to what we might call his "cosmic morale," and it challenges him to revise fundamentally his entire world view.

Having considered the possible extent of man's historical mastery, let us consider the means. Here perhaps the most important question has to do with the role of violence.

27

Can serious injustices ordinarily be corrected without violence?

The two main sides of this question are represented in typical views of liberals and of radicals.

Liberals believe in the possibility of correcting injustice through persuasion. The concept of this possibility, indeed, is one of the essential principles making up the liberal ideal. Everyone has the right to speak freely and to join with others of like mind in promulgating his views; by virtue of this right everyone can bring his grievances to the attention of the government and the citizens. The critical point is that one can anticipate a reasonable hearing, which means not only that his grievances will be fairly considered but that action will be taken to alleviate them if it is necessary. That is one reason why liberty is practical and desirable: It offers a way of peacefully correcting injustice.

Liberals thus are optimistic both as to ends and as to means; the most serious injustices can finally be eliminated, and this can be done without violence.

Radicals, on the other hand, typically doubt the effectiveness of persuasion where important interests are at stake. Marx, for example, did not expect capitalists in most places voluntarily to give up their holdings. While suggesting that the proletariat might in one or two countries come to power peacefully, he thought that in most countries violence would be unavoidable.

Radicals thus are optimistic as to ends but pessimistic as to means. They believe, as do liberals, that injustice finally will be conquered; but they do not expect this to come about through mutual agreement. It is a measure of the seriousness of injustice, at least of economic injustice (if we are speaking of Marx and his followers), that it divides human beings so that they cannot perceive one another's interests or enter into common discussion.

The difference between liberals and radicals probably arises partly from differing appraisals of violence. A liberal is apt to regard violence as a uniquely evil form of power. Not that he rules it out without any regard whatever for circumstances, as do anarchists and pacifists. But he is apt to feel that it is far more subversive of decent relationships than most of the other ways in which some people get others to conform with their will; violence is worse, for example, than propaganda or economic pressure. It must therefore be used only as a last resort.

Radicals usually are less wary of violence. In the long run, to be sure, they look forward to a great lessening or even to the total disappearance of violence; they are likely also to be vehement in their condemnations of the repressive violence used by the dominant classes. For the typical radical, however, the propaganda and the economic pressures employed by these classes are morally no better than open violence; as for those underneath, who are resisting, they need not worry that the integrity of their cause will be compromised by the violence they will be compelled to use.

Most radicals would go at least this far; some would go farther. There is a kind of radicalism in which violence, when used for revolutionary purposes by oppressed people, is seen as a positive good. It is a proof of humanity. Only human beings can violently rebel; in doing so, therefore, they prove that they are not mere things, to be used as others desire.

There is something more decisive beneath the liberal-radical split concerning the use of violence, however, than a difference concerning the morality of violence. That is a difference concerning man and his nature.

Liberals characteristically see human beings, at least in the vast majority, as reasonable. They see them as reasonable both in beliefs and in actions; that is, people not only use reason — and use it competently — in arriving at their beliefs, but also they shape their conduct in the light of these rational beliefs. This is why persuasion can be upheld as the best way of attacking injustice.

Radicals do not ordinarily dispute the proposition that man is reasonable in essence; their long-range hopes usually depend on the assumption that he is. But they are apt to hold that the realization of this rational essence is thwarted under the conditions created by serious injustice. This is why persuasion cannot be expected to work. Marx is illustrative of this point of view. He believed that human beings were reasonable enough for social and economic life finally, after the consolidation of the communist revolution, to be brought wholly under the governance of reason, with violence disappearing; but he certainly did not believe that capitalists were reasonable, except in the narrow sense of rationally pursuing their own selfish interests. They were not reasonable enough to understand either the nature of the common good or the laws of economic development, in Marx's opinion. Why not? Simply because their minds were confined by their circumstances. Capitalists were capable of being rational about their own interests, Marx held, but not about the needs of mankind.

Many radicals adhere to some such determinism as this. Serious injustices cannot ordinarily be corrected without violence because they are destructive of rationality. They establish divisions that reason cannot surmount.

In a manner of speaking, the question is whether everyone lives in a single universe. It is hardly too much to say that they do not, as seen by many radicals; at least they do not for the time being. In Marxism, for example, workers and capitalists live completely differently from one another; they do not have similar philosophies, similar emotions, or similar ends. And not only are their circumstances and attitudes disparate; their interests are diametrically in conflict. As a result of these conditions, they cannot possibly communicate with one another, and it is not much of an exaggeration to speak of their inhabiting separate universes. Some radicals have placed equally drastic emphasis on the division between blacks and whites. Their experiences and their interests are so completely different that reason is helpless in relation to the issues that divide them.

Liberals (although not liberals alone) persistently reject such dichotomies. Human beings are never so distant from one another that they do not still share a single universe of reason, in the liberal view. Hence never can it be taken for granted that discussion is useless and violence inevitable.

Anyone who wishes carefully to reflect on this issue should be aware that it concerns not only the nature of man in general but also the nature of reason. I have stated the issue as though reasonableness included concern for the interests of others; it has been assumed that a reasonable man is one who can talk with others because he is capable of understanding and respecting their concerns. In short, reason is in part a moral faculty. To look on reason in this way is in the tradition of liberalism. There is, however, another concept of reason, and even those who reject it should be prepared to take it into account.

It is possible to hold that reason is nothing more than a faculty for engaging in means-ends calculations, a faculty having nothing to do with morality. A reasonable man is merely one who is skilled in devising ways of fulfilling his own interests, whether or not his interests coincide with the interests of others. From this point of view reason does not disclose the ideal order within which all of us should live; it is merely, as Hume remarked, the "slave of the passions."

Deciding this particular issue does not decide the overall issue we are discussing; as is readily apparent, however, it does have an important bearing on it.

Now, having reflected on questions concerning both the possible extent and the requisite means of deliberate historical change, let us consider its significance. The primary question we face here is whether historical changes determine the whole framework of human life. Are one's relations with other human beings and with the universe totally subject to history? Or is there a changeless structure of right and truth that a moral and rational being can inhabit regardless of what happens in history? It would be reassuring to think that there is, that certain standards and truths, at least, are not engulfed in history. A number of thinkers, however, would deny this reassurance. All realities, all principles, all moral rules are mutable. Thus everything is submerged in the flow of events, and the futility and tragedy of history encompass the whole world in which man lives. Is this true?

28

Do truth and right change in the course of history?

It may be doubted whether all of those who answer this question affirmatively — "standards change," they assert — are altogether ready to live in the kind of universe to which they thus commit themselves. It may be doubted, in other words, that they are fully aware of what they are saying. If truth and right really do change in the course of history, then it would seem that there are no fixed points in relation to which one's life can be organized and guided. Liberty, democracy, justice, respect for life, honesty — every rule one might rely on for conducting his life and appraising his surroundings gives way. And not only right and wrong, but reality itself dissolves and is carried away in the flux of events. One cannot hold to "human nature" or to any other rock. Indeed, if one takes with full seriousness the idea that all basic principles change in the course of history, he will find even that idea itself escaping like water through his fingers, for it too must be one of those principles that changes in the course of time.

The contemporary French writer and thinker, Jean-Paul Sartre, has written a novel entitled *Nausea.* In this book he depicts with great dramatic force the vertigo and horror felt by a man who begins to perceive the realities around him as completely lacking any firm structure or meaning. Nothing, not even the chair on which one is sitting, not even one's own hand, has a clear form or purpose. Such a molten, meaningless universe is literally sickening, and hence the title of Sartre's book.

Those for whom "standards change," and for whom that is an absolutely serious and final judgment, live in a universe that is like a ship in heavy seas; the objects around one all are unfixed or straining to break away, the deck presses upward beneath one's feet or plunges away unexpectedly, and even the horizon seems to move. Such, perhaps, is truly the human situation. If so, it is not something to celebrate; as Sartre saw, what one naturally feels is nausea.

Thus it is not surprising that men have always tried to find ground above the flood of change and that political thinkers have sought principles of human relations that will not crumble and disappear in the stream of history. Indeed, it is hardly too much to say that political philosophy began with an effort to find firm ground. Plato as a young man saw the dissolution not only of Athenian political institutions but also of Hellenic moral and religious convictions. Athenian governments were repeatedly overthrown, and the city was filled with men who said, and who acted as though they believed, that there were no fixed standards of morality. Plato's response can be found in *The Republic.* The central argument of that work is that the basis of political order, and of all valid and fulfilling life, is an understanding of what is always true and always good.

But what *is* always true and always good? Plato's famous "doctrine of forms" represented an effort to answer this question. Every reality — every man, tree, chair, or rock — is real only because it participates in a universal, changeless form — the form of a man, a tree, a chair, or a rock. These forms, for Plato, were what we might call "ideas" or "essences." They could not be seen or touched, but were absolutely real and could be known intellectually. "The Good," which we have already discussed, may be thought of as the form of all forms and thus as the eternal source of being and of value. What is most important in the context of the present discussion is that Plato envisioned the forms as neither coming into being nor passing away, as having no history and as unaffected by history.

The philosopher, as Plato imagined him, dwelt in the world of forms. He had ascended from the world of things that are seen and touched to the forms, and from the forms to the Good. He had in this way ascended from the changing to the lasting and had risen above history. Were he to rule absolutely, then a whole city might be founded on a plane above the violence and confusion of historical change.

Readers of *The Republic* may feel that Plato's fear of change was extreme. Plato's general outlook, however, is not unique and even in his own time was not novel. Plato took up a search that had already been initiated by other philosophers and that has continued to our own day, a search for what often is referred to simply as "nature." I have already briefly discussed the ancient issue of nature versus convention. One of the most notable features of this controversy is that convention has had so few defenders, while the idea of nature has for millenia had a remarkable and only occasionally questioned authority. One of the principal reasons for this seems to be that nature, that is, the fundamental structure of being, does not change; such as least, has been the prevailing belief.

The concept of nature underlies what is probably the most durable and powerful idea in the whole history of Western moral and political thought — natural law. This is the idea (in its essence) that human relations are subject to a law that is discernible by reason and unaffected by historical change. Times and customs may change, but the principles governing human relations remain the same. Some of our most civilized institutions, such as personal liberties, democratic government, and international law and organization, can be traced back to this idea. If this one timber in the structure of our civilization were withdrawn, we might suddenly find ourselves standing in the midst of ruins.

Even the ancient Hebrews, with their profound historical consciousness, sought a standpoint above the flux of history. In general, they were far less fearful of change and far less inclined to see it as a sign of unreality than were the ancient Greeks. Even Jehovah (although in some ways it would be more accurate to say *particularly* Jehovah) was outside of any fixed and knowable order; his decisions were free and unforeseeable, and he is represented occasionally even as repenting of things he has done. As for man and the rest of creation, here too the Hebrews differed from the Greeks; they did not share the typical Hellenic belief that reality is basically an inalterable rational order.

With all of this, the Hebrews still affirmed that some things were beyond historical change. "The mercy of the Lord is from everlasting to everlasting," and one expression of this mercy is the Law, the commandments given to Moses on Mount Sinai. These cannot be touched by any process of historical erosion. In this way the Hebrews, like the Greeks, grounded society on an unchanging order.

The quest for inalterable realities and rules has been pressed so persistently that one feels in it the expression of a basic imperative of human existence. It seems that we can hardly live if nothing endures. Nevertheless, the last two centuries have witnessed numerous attacks on "nature" and natural law. As for nature (what *is*, as distinguished from what *ought* to be) some of the most profound and persuasive philosophers have argued against the notion that there is a knowable, permanent structure of being. Hume did so in maintaining the thesis that no necessary connection links cause and effect. When we speak of cause and effect, according to Hume, we merely report recurrent sequences in our sensations. We have no way of knowing whether the sequences that held in the past will continue to hold in the future. Hence we can make no assertions concerning the basic order of reality; we cannot even know that there is such an order. A similar view is implicit in the works of Kant, despite his intention of refuting Hume. One of the main themes of *The Critique of Pure Reason* is that the changeless structure men thought they had discovered in nature is imposed by the mind and does not hold among the "things-in-themselves."

The idea that reality is essentially a fixed natural order was challenged from another angle by Henri Bergson (1859–1941), whose popularity has somewhat declined but who was a thinker of great originality and eloquence. According to Bergson, change is not only real; it is the very essence of reality. "There do not exist *things* made, but only things in the making, not *states* that remain fixed, but only states in process of change." [4] This is most obvious in respect to living things and to man. Bergson admitted that some realities are relatively

[4] Henri Bergson, *The Creative Mind: An Introduction to Metaphysics* (New York: Philosophical Library, 1946), p. 188. The italics are Bergson's.

fixed, but these are dead and inorganic, not alive and spiritual. The quest for the changeless was something he condemned. He saw it as an effort to impose the fixity which is alone fitted to the grasp of our minds on what is intrinsically "unceasing creation."

A final example of the modern attack on natural order is existentialism. One way of stating the theme uniting the various forms of existentialism is by saying that human nature is not a changeless, transhistorical form. Man is free, or subjective, and thus beyond every fixed, objective principle.

The question we are considering concerns not only truth but also right. What about right? So far as views of the kind we have just been discussing prevail, the belief in changeless moral principles tends to decline. Kant showed, to be sure, that this is not an invariable rule; although attacking the usual objectivist concept of nature, he set forth a moral theory that has become almost notorious for its rigid and uncompromising conception of duty. But the traditional ideal of natural law necessarily falls if there is no nature. Hume founded morality on the wants and propensities of the individual, as well as on custom and habit; for Bergson, a good act was a creative act, arising from an intuitive sense of the movement of life; existentialists have typically argued that choice creates values rather than being subordinated to values. None of these thinkers argued that something was good merely because an individual or a society called it good; they were not total relativists. All, however, reflected the decay of the ancient conviction that certain moral standards remain despite all historical change.

A good example of the prevalent view that the right is relative to time and place is the thought of Marx. Much of the force of Marx's writing lay in his apparent demonstration that many realities and standards that had been regarded as part of the inalterable order of nature, such as the profit motive, private property, and government by parliaments, were in actuality merely the beliefs and customs of a particular historical era and were destined to disappear. Marx as a man was not without absolute moral standards, as is plain in the bitterness of his denunciations of callous employers. As a thinker, however, he had no such standards. His aim was not to show that capitalist civilization was evil but that it was temporary. His revolutionary power comes from the skill and thoroughness with which he swept all aspects of the civilization he hated into the torrent of history.

Is it merely a sign of weakness in man that for so many centuries he tried to ground society on the changeless — on eternal forms, on "nature," or on God? Or is it because of an intuition that relationships without such a foundation can have no substance or validity?

With questions like these we are groping our way amid the shadows of contemporary despair. We have little confidence in the course of history, and we are afraid that our being and our relationships are wholly at the disposal of a merciless and capricious history.

But is history really so cruel and so unreliable? Perhaps it is less malignant and irrational in its ultimate ends than appears on the surface. It may be, in other words, that the natural and moral order which sometimes seems to be dissolved in history is, in actuality, being created by history and thus is the innermost logic of the historical process.

These hypotheses define roughly the course of modern thought. Having come to doubt that truth and right are invulnerable to history, and having thus given up the ancient and medieval faith that there is an eternal and changeless order of nature underlying historical change, modern man tried to find truth and right in the structure and purpose of history itself. This effort produced some ingenious and fascinating conceptions of the historical process. Here we shall confine ourselves to the most general form of the idea; this is simply the doctrine of progress. To hold that history tends to produce a better life — better in the sense not merely of being more comfortable but also of being more reasonable and humane — is to hold both that history is rational, because it is a process leading toward a desirable end and also, and for the same reason, that it is moral. Truth and right thus regain the primacy that they seemed, for a moment, to have lost; it turns out that they determine the logic of the very historical process that threatened them.

But is the doctrine of progress valid?

29

Does history lead naturally toward a better life?

For some generations modern man has answered with an exuberant "Yes." Progress has been taken to be a natural, if not inevitable, characteristic of human history. A typical and influential representative of this view is Antoine-Nicolas de Condorcet (1743–1794). The core idea in Condorcet's philosophy of history is the limitless perfectibility of man. In maintaining this principle, Condorcet meant not only that man *may* become perfect, which Rousseau, an opponent of the doctrine of progress, also believed; he meant, too, that man has a strong bent toward perfection and that history, as a result, tends naturally toward the realization of this perfection.

The key to progress, for Condorcet, lay in rational enlightenment. Science extends and deepens knowledge; printing and education spread it. It is assumed, in Socratic fashion, that growth in knowledge must be accompanied by growth in moral excellence. Condorcet admitted that the path of progress might lead through distressing times. He looked back on the Middle Ages, for example, as a period of superstition, intolerance, and priestly oppression. But he seems to have had little fear that man might descend forever into an era of darkness. He saw the human race as moved by a nearly irresistible destiny toward enlightenment, and through enlightenment toward universal freedom and equality.

Among other well-known exponents of progress in recent times are Hegel and Marx. One can see in both thinkers the modern inclination to believe in progress regardless of what the determining force of history is thought to be. Neither attributed preponderant influence to conscious will or to knowledge. For Hegel ideas, for Marx economic forces, ordered the march of affairs. They assumed that at certain points in the unfoldment of history these had to be recognized, thus entering into the conscious determination of events; but for long periods of time they might shape events despite the ignorance and resistance of participants. They thought that progress, over the long run, was inevitable. The blindness and inadequacies of human beings might delay it but could not completely block it.

The authority of the idea of progress is particularly evident in the Hegelian and Marxist "dialectic." Both thinkers believed that progress comes about, so to speak, in a "zig-zag" fashion rather than in a straight line. Progress is not a steady and harmonious forward movement. It comes about through tension and conflict, and the most catastrophic moments may presage the most glorious ones. The fact that human beings are usually backward-looking and confused, therefore, is not an obstruction on the road of history. Far from inhibiting progress, error and conflict are among the devices by which progress is accomplished.

Assurance of the ascendant course of history could hardly be more emphatically affirmed. Whether through ideas or through economic forces, whether by means of the resistance of participants or by means of their cooperation, the law of progress maintains its sway.

However, just as I had to point out before that belief in man's power to direct history is more than counterbalanced by the older and more enduring conviction that history is determined by some power beyond man, so here it is necessary to say that the doctrine of progress, although very popular during the last century or two, is far from expressing the consensus of Western thinkers. On the contrary, the history of thought reflects a great deal of pessimism about the course of events. For example, the ancient Greeks and Romans generally assumed that history moves through more or less regular cycles; recurrence, rather than progress, was seen as the law of history.

It is easy to understand how such an idea might arise. Recurrence is a pronounced and even awesome characteristic of man's environment and life. It occurs in the changing of the seasons and in the passing of the generations. But while the idea of historical cycles is in this sense comprehensible, it expresses a mood very far from the hopefulness of Condorcet and other apostles of progress. If history is cyclical, then ultimately nothing is accomplished. There may be achievements within a single cycle, but the long ages of history, comprising many cycles, can be nothing more than the recurrent restoration and decay of what was achieved in the first cycle. A terrible futility reigns in human affairs.

Augustine and other Christian thinkers repudiated the cyclical concept of history. They had to. Otherwise the life of Christ, as well as all other acts of God, would have fallen under the law and have been cursed by the absurdity of endless repetition. However, the alternative view developed by Christian thinkers also was markedly pessimistic.

Among orthodox Christians history was envisioned as leading toward a finale of suffering and terror: "For nation shall rise against nation, and kingdom against kingdom: and there shall be earthquakes in divers places, and there shall be famines and troubles." [5] With the end of history, of course, God would establish his Kingdom, and this climax, to which all of the ages since Adam's sin had been leading, would give history a meaning such as it could not have were it governed by the law of cyclical recurrence. History was, then, leading toward a better life. It was not, however, leading toward a better *earthly* life; the Kingdom of God was conceived to be, in its perfection, unlike any earthly kingdom. Nor was history leading *naturally* toward a better life; it was leading naturally, that is, under the impetus of iniquitous men, toward catastrophe, and only the intervention of God turned it into a process of redemption.

Thus it is plain that while history has a purpose and meaning in the Christian vision that it cannot have in the classical mind where it is conceived as cyclical, there is an immense chasm between the Christian view of history and the modern doctrine of progress. In the Christian view, the beginning is the moral suicide of man; in the doctrine of progress, man loses his way but not his fundamental innocence. In the Christian view, the dominant motif is tragedy, and man must anticipate "affliction, such as was not from the beginning of the creation which God created unto this time"; [6] in the doctrine of progress, the major theme is steady improvement. In the Christian vision, the end is a transfiguration of reality in which the earth, as we know it, vanishes; according to the doctrine of

[5] Mark 13:8.
[6] Mark 13:19.

progress, we may look toward increasing harmony and happiness on this earth.

Christianity suggests another reason as well for questioning the doctrine of progress. This is the idea that ultimately nothing is significant except the loss and the redemption of individual souls. "For what is a man profited, if he shall gain the whole world, and lose his own soul." [7] From this point of view all progress must be spiritual and personal; thus it becomes questionable whether any historical, as distinguished from personal, development can be seriously considered as progressive or otherwise. What does anyone seeking his own redemption care about the course and the end of history?

It is important to note that this perspective is not uniquely Christian, although it is suggested by Christianity. In its most general form it consists simply in the notion that everything must be judged by its effect on individuals; only individuals — never historical events — are "ends in themselves." Doubt thus is cast on the whole idea of progress, even from a materialistic point of view; for the increasing convenience and comfort men enjoy can never justify the squalor and misery in which countless multitudes have passed their lives. The idea of progress is challenged with particular sharpness if the individual is treated as a moral and spiritual being, as one who is not necessarily better off merely because he is more comfortable.

If morality is a matter of personal choice, and if spirituality depends on occurrences within the soul of the individual, it is not clear how an age, as distinguished from a person, can be morally and spiritually ahead of or behind another age. Can historical conditions place individuals on moral and spiritual levels that they would fall below under other conditions? If so, then moral and spiritual greatness are apparently merely products of external circumstances, not of personal striving. Reflection along these lines can lead one to wonder whether the nineteenth and twentieth centuries, with all of their self-satisfaction, have achieved any genuine progress at all.

In other words, when thinking of historical progress, we seem to be thinking of vast multitudes of human beings and

[7] Matthew 16:26.

little of the individual. When we think of the individual, on the other hand, then the significance of the multitudes that constitute historical eras becomes problematic.

Today, we do not know what to think about the natural course of history any more than we do about the question of how far history is under human control. And our doubts in both cases are the result of the unexpected disasters that have befallen mankind since 1914. The idea of progress has suddenly come to seem old-fashioned and unrealistic. But what can we put in place of it? We do not appear to have the kind of faith that would be required to return to the Christian idea that history ends with the destruction of the world and the establishment of a heavenly kingdom, although many sense an apocalyptic quality in the nuclear cloud. As for the cyclical concept of history, that strikes us as no less implausible, and intolerable as well. It is implausible because for two millenia we have been taught that history had a direction and a purpose. Further, in the past two centuries we have seen events like industrialization that we know have never happened before; these events seem to disprove any theory of cyclical recurrence. The cyclical view is intolerable because, after believing for so long that history is purposeful, we are crushed by the thought that it is merely endless, useless repetition.

In James Joyce's novel *Ulysses* someone says that history is a nightmare from which he is trying to awake.[8] This remark expresses the mood of historical insecurity and fear that has been created in many people today by half a century of disorder and violence. It expresses the mood that must descend on those who have confidence neither in their own control of history nor in the beneficence of its natural tendencies. If we can neither control nor trust the course of events, it is difficult not to feel that the universe is like a capricious despot who may at any time wreck our relationships and our lives. Personal life is burdened by the impression that the surrounding universe is senseless; political life is demoralized by the feeling that the consequences of any action are incalculable and menacing.

Thus we find ourselves challenged by the question we would

[8] James Joyce, *Ulysses* (New York: The Modern Library, 1914), p. 35.

like to dismiss as an invitation to useless, metaphysical dreams: Has history any meaning?

Beyond this, we find ourselves challenged by a particularly annoying subsidiary question, and that is whether history has a meaning that is *not* derived from anything within history itself — that *is* derived, in other words, from the transcendent.

Here we encounter doubts of the kind referred to at the outset of this chapter, doubts that "take one's breath away." I would not deny that we scarcely know what we mean when we ask such questions. On the other hand, I do not see how we can responsibly avoid them.

SUGGESTED READINGS

(Titles are listed chronologically. All are available in paperback or other inexpensive editions.)

Saint Augustine. *The City of God*
Hegel, Georg Wilhelm Friedrich. *The Philosophy of History*
Marx, Karl, and Engels, Friedrich. *The Communist Manifesto*
Dostoevsky, Fyodor. *The Possessed*
Sorel, Georges. *Reflections on Violence*
Bury, J. B. *The Idea of Progress*
Berdyaev, Nicholas. *The Meaning of History*
Popper, Karl. *The Open Society and Its Enemies*, 2 vols.
Löwith, Karl. *Meaning in History*
Niebuhr, Reinhold. *The Irony of American History*
Frankel, Charles. *The Case for Modern Man*
Bultman, Rudolf. *History and Eschatology: The Presence of Eternity*
Fanon, Frantz. *The Wretched of the Earth*
Arendt, Hannah. *On Revolution*
Ellul, Jacques. *Autopsy of Revolution*

Epilogue: The Idea
of Humane Uncertainty

How can one keep from intellectual despair in the face of questions that for twenty-five centuries have defied the efforts of philosophers to find demonstrable, universally acceptable answers? To show that there are perennial questions about politics may serve to rebut heedless votaries of religious dogma or of science who assume that no great questions remain unanswered. However, it may only fortify those who shun political speculation not because they assume the great questions have already been answered but because they assume they can never be answered.

To counter such despair it may be in order here to remind the reader of two points suggested in Chapter 1 and to probe somewhat more deeply into those points than seemed appropriate before the reader had gained experience in political speculation.

The first point is that answers are possible. It is true that they cannot be established so surely and finally as are scientific laws; the failure of political thinkers to reach agreement in twenty-five centuries of speculation shows that this is so. But the history of thought is not completely discouraging, for it shows that human beings repeatedly overcome their uncertainties and take positions with assurance.

How can this be done? How is it possible for an intelligent person to take with assurance a philosophical position that he knows is not objectively certain? This is a mysterious spiritual event, and it would not be feasible in a book of this kind to try fully to explain it. Perhaps it is in order, however, for me briefly to sketch a possible explanation.

To begin with, it seems that a philosophical idea is the symbol of an inner state that is something different from and independent of the idea. Plato's concept of the philosopher-king, for example, symbolized a vision of men at one with the source of being and with other men. One gains only a glimmering of this vision by comprehending and joining the words "philosopher" and "king." The idea and the vision are not the same, although both have reference to the same ultimate reality.

If this is so, one may recognize the uncertainty of an idea even while remaining sure of the vision that it represents. Still, this suggestion is apt to strike the reader as unsatisfactory. Presumably an idea must be either true or false. How can an idea represent the truth and yet not be literally true?

Certain ideas of Kant's may help us to reflect on this question. According to Kant, knowledge in the strictest sense of the term, that is, knowledge that does not just point to the truth but is literally true, pertains to objects. Now an object is not just any reality but is a reality that exists in space and time and within the causal order. In other words, it is of the essence of an object that it be one among a plurality of objects and that it bear a determinate relationship to those objects, through its location in space and time and its place in the causal order.

On this basis, and still following Kant, let us try to understand more deeply the nature of objects. They derive their character as objects, according to what has just been said, from the framework in which they exist — a framework constituted primarily by space and time and by causal relationships. From what does this framework, in turn, derive? According to Kant, it derives from man's mind. Space and time, as well as causal relationships, are forms we impose on our perceptions. We are compelled to employ these forms if we are to have any coherent experience; otherwise we would confront nothing more than a chaos of sensations.

What would happen to objects if they were removed from this framework? They would disappear. One cannot even speak of an object outside of the spatio-temporal and causal framework. It is precisely inclusion within that framework that turns otherwise evanescent and meaningless sensations into experience and knowledge.

This all may strike the reader as reasonable enough but perhaps not particularly significant. When Kant's position is fully assimilated, however, it can mean a kind of liberation — a liberation from the basically materialistic conviction, which seems to many people at present to be mere common sense, that every reality must be some kind of thing, or object, and that the whole universe can be nothing more than a vast collection of things. The implication of Kant's argument is that an object is formed by the mind and does not have independent reality. The same is true of the whole world, of the totality of objects: It is no more than the perceptual and intellectual framework that we impose on the sensations that come to us.

In this way the hard and often oppressive things that surround us lose their totalitarian command over our minds. It is not that we can wholly deny their reality or ignore them in our daily lives. But we do not have to assume that everything that is real is cut to their pattern.

This is to say that objective knowledge of the kind that attains its greatest perfection in the physical sciences ceases to be our one sure means of access to reality. Indeed, such knowledge does not pertain to ultimate reality. This does not mean that it lacks importance. Within its own realm, that of appearance, it has unshakable authority. But it does not comprise being-in-itself.

Thus certain ultimate objects of inquiry, realities that man has persistently striven to understand, are not even, in principle, objects of knowledge. More succinctly, they are not objects. Thus the world as a whole, which we automatically envision as a kind of all-inclusive object which we ought to be able to know just as we know any other object, turns out to be simply the way we organize our experience. The world is the context of objects, but not itself an object. Accordingly, anyone who conceives of knowing the world as a whole, in the same fashion in which we know objects, is proceeding on the basis of a fundamental misunderstanding.

God is another example of a reality, or a possible reality, that men have long striven to know but that turns out to be not even in principle an object of knowledge. Perhaps the main reason so many people today feel that there is *obviously* no God lies in the assumption that every reality must be some kind of object. If this assumption were well founded, then atheism would be inevitable, for it is plain that no object — that is, nothing that is within space and time, and thus finite, and nothing that is causally determined from without — can be God. In challenging the identification of reality and objectivity Kant reopens for modern man the whole question of divine reality. In limiting reason, Kant asserted, he made room for faith.

One other reality, in addition to the world as a whole and God, that man has sought persistently to understand is man himself. Where does man, as an ultimate object of inquiry, stand after the Kantian revolution? It would be impossible in a few lines to do justice to Kant's obscure and complex theory concerning our knowledge of man. Suffice it to say that not only is man something more than an object of knowledge; he is in a special position in that, as mind, he is the source of the whole world of objects. He is not completely unknowable, for he does have a body and a psychic mechanism that can be studied through science. These are only appearances of man, however, not man as he is in himself.

How does all of this relate to the problem before us — understanding how it is possible to reach inner assurance on the basis of doctrines one knows to be objectively uncertain? Briefly, by showing that our doctrines, through representing ultimate realities, can possess a kind of truth even though in their literal meanings they are very much open to doubt.

Kant's philosophy makes it possible to think that the "inner state" or "vision" that may be represented by an idea like the philosopher-king, is an immediate contact with being; as such, it would be an insight going beyond objective knowledge and penetrating, as it were, into the ultimate reality of which objects are mere appearances. This is only a hypothesis. What recommends it, however, is that it helps us to understand how an idea can be significant and put us in touch with reality, without being literally true. An idea does this when it reminds us of, or evokes in us, a consciousness of ultimate reality, even though that consciousness cannot be put into words and set forth as objective truth.

In short, something inexpressible, and in that sense subjective, is spoken of here as though it were objective. Realization of a reality that is beyond the objects around us is put in terms that we use primarily to apply to those objects.

What justification is there for this? What right have we to speak of nonobjective realities, like the world as a whole and man, as though they were objective realities? Here again Kant can help us. He enables us to perceive that our words are fitted for objects and therefore, that being itself defies all of the resources of language. We can speak with precision about the things around us but not about the ultimate realities behind them; we can phrase exactly our knowledge, but not our wisdom, or our vision. This leaves us with just two possibilities. We can, as one contemporary thinker has advised, "pass over in silence" all of those matters that we cannot speak of precisely and objectively. Or else we can speak of those nonobjective realities as though they were objective. Kant, although not unequivocally, advocates the latter course.

This may all be rather hard to understand. In offering such brief remarks on so perplexing a subject I hope only to give the reader an idea as to how it might be that one is inwardly assured although outwardly uncertain, and as to how the answers that we reach through reflection may possess value and even a kind of truth, while having no claim to being final, demonstrable knowledge.

We should note, however, that while this possibility is perplexing when we reflect on it, we commonly assume that it is real. We often use words like "vision," "insight," and "wisdom." Most of us assume that these words designate some kind of understanding, but not the kind of understanding that is gained through exact, demonstrable knowledge. Most of us also assume that those possessing wisdom, or other such qualities, can communicate in words, even though their words cannot have the same kind of literal accuracy as the words of scientists. This assumption shows that in our everyday thinking we acknowledge the distinction between the literal meaning and the ultimate bearing of the ideas that we hold. It shows also that the notion that we may understand something, and understand it assuredly and deeply, even though every statement we make about it is challengeable and uncertain, is not far from common sense.

The second point to which we may appropriately return, in view of the apparent hopelessness of answering definitively the great questions of political thought, is closely allied with the first one. It is that there is a kind of truth in the very process of thought, apart from any answers that it reaches. The act of thinking in itself is an opening up of reality — at the very least, as suggested in Chapter 1, the reality of the self as a being capable of standing aside and questioning and the reality of others as potential companions in inquiry.

Where few principles have been developed, as in the early stages of human society, much of reality must remain in darkness. On the other hand, where many principles have been developed, but with little sense of their incompleteness, of their uncertainty, and of the gap between a principle and the reality it symbolizes, then reality is frozen in an icy, uncomprehending certitude. For example, persons, with their capacity for diverging from all predictions, are hidden behind dogmas. This has often happened among religious believers and among devotees of science (often not scientists themselves), although neither religion nor science necessarily entails such dogmatism. Only through thinking, in which principles are apprehended but are also questioned, can we enter into the presence of reality.

I suggest, in sum, that wisdom is not gained by answering questions in a way that leaves the questions forever behind but in establishing a thoughtful and continuing relationship to questions. Wisdom is a thinking state.

This humane uncertainty is not without political meaning. For one thing, from awareness of my own power of asking questions arises an intuition that any organization or authority that attempts to suppress my questions and to make me a mere thoughtless and automatic part of some monolithic group, like a totalitarian state, violates my essential being. An act of thought is a kind of declaration of freedom, and to be serious about reflection is to be incapable of slavery or subservience.

Further, the experience of questioning carries an intuition not only of freedom but also of equality. One person may know more about mathematics or automobile engines or history than another, but before the perennial questions we are all, in our lack of definite, demonstrable answers, equal. The wise stand above others, it would seem, only in their consciousness of this primal equality.

At this point, however, we encounter a serious question — a question that we must briefly consider, even though it will be impossible for us to settle it. On what final premise does the resolute pursuit of truth, with its openness to communication, rest? We have not really probed so deeply as it might seem. I have suggested that answers to one's questions are possible and that there is truth of a sort in the very act of thought. Are these the ultimate premises of political thinking? The question is important because, while wisdom may be a thinking state, the converse is not true: Not always is a thinking state wisdom. It may bring instead enervating doubt or even nihilism, an attack on all values. Through what kind of underlying faith can these consequences be avoided?

Thinking along these lines, forcing ourselves deeper than we have so far gone, two further premises suggest themselves. The first is that truth is good. "Truth" is one of those words that we often capitalize and often take to represent something so obviously sublime that we need not consider its value. But it is possible, after all, to think that the ultimate truth may prove not to be very interesting or even to be harmful. If it should be, for example, that the structure of reality is fundamentally antithetical to human interests, then illusions might be not only far pleasanter than the truth but essential if mankind is not to be suffocated under a blanket of hopelessness.

The second additional premise is not required simply for thinking, but it is required for thinking in the only fashion that most of us would approve of — in a way that is open to all and is not merely an activity of a privileged few. This premise is that every person is a potential and rightful participant in inquiry. It is possible, after all, to hold that most people are too unintelligent and frivolous to engage in serious reflective inquiry, and that in any case they have no rights along those lines: Those of us engaged in inquiry have no obligation to open this activity up to everyone.

In short, in setting forth to think, I must have respect both for truth and for persons.

Here we reach the final question: On what does such respect depend?

Many today would say that it depends on nothing at all and that one has here reached the ultimate grounds of serious and open inquiry. This must, in essence, be the position of atheists: Nothing is more ultimate than truth and the individual human being.

Perhaps this position is sound. It does, however, leave room for serious doubts. Why should we look upon truth as an ultimate value, regardless of the nature of reality? In the history of thought truth has usually, albeit not invariably, been a religious value; reverence for truth has expressed reverence for being, with being regarded either as divine in itself or as expressive of the divine. Such a view is logical and understandable, even though one may dispute its religious presuppositions. But is it logical or understandable to retain reverence for the truth after the divine has been denied?

The idea that every individual is a potential and rightful participant in inquiry can be questioned in a similar fashion. It is true, as noted above, that we are all equal in our inability to answer definitively the perennial questions. But does this suffice for justifying inquiry that is open to all? It may be argued that while no one possesses definitive answers to the perennial questions, the ability to reflect on these questions and to find the wisdom to which reflection sometimes leads is confined to a few. In reaction to so elitist a view, the reader may assert that there is a dignity in every individual, regardless of his intellectual abilities or interests, and that this entitles him to be admitted into an activity so essential to our humanity as is philosophical inquiry. Aside from the question of whether such admission is even possible, however, it can be argued, as brought out in connection with Question 4, that the idea of a dignity inhering in each individual is no less religious in its presuppositions than is the idea that truth is good. On the basis of empirical, dispassionate analysis, it may be said, there is no more reason to accord respect to every human being than there is to accord respect to every horse or every automobile.

The question I am raising can be summarily restated. To enter seriously into inquiry that is open to all expresses substantial faith in the universe, in being. Truth is good, and all persons have the right and the potentiality to share in the search for it. Does this faith make sense if its final object is only what we can see and know, rather than God?

The question can be underscored by noting that it arises as well from the assumption underlying most of this Epilogue, that truth is accessible. I have argued that reflection can lead us to answers, and that even apart from these answers it opens up reality. How can we be sure, however, that this process does not occur within the boundaries of some all-encompassing illusion in which we are confined by the very nature of reality and of our own minds and from which we cannot possibly escape? Further, even if truth is accessible, how can we have the courage to seek it in the face of the total and everlasting oblivion that death seems to promise us?

Again it becomes apparent that serious inquiry is an act of faith. And again it can be asked: Faith in what?

Rather than prolonging what has already been a long series of demands on the reader's willingness to labor in the rarefied atmosphere of philosophical abstraction, let me conclude with a concrete example. The ideal of humane uncertainty is exemplified by a great historical figure, Socrates — the ugly, amiable, and devastatingly intelligent Athenian, who was finally put to death for his uncompromising pursuit of inquiry. Apparently Socrates did not expound a complete and definite doctrine but concentrated instead on asking questions about such matters as courage and friendship and justice. He devoted his whole mature life to the discussion of these questions. Although he was particularly interested in talking with men who had reputations for wisdom, he seems always to have gladly entered into discourse with any willing participant whom he happened to encounter. He concluded at the end of his life that no one could answer his questions and that those who were reputed to be wise were in reality ignorant. It was the fact that this conclusion emerged irresistibly from Socrates's life and that it humiliated and threatened some of the most eminent men in Athens, that led ultimately to his trial and execution.

Two aspects of Socrates's life are particularly noteworthy in relation to the ideal of humane uncertainty. One is that Socrates concluded not only that all others were ignorant but that he himself was ignorant. He was superior to others, he held, only in his awareness of his own ignorance. Thus on the face of things Socrates was a failure. A lifetime of questioning had led him to no answers. It had led him only to a point at which he was so hated and mistrusted by his fellow Athenians that they condemned him to death for introducing spiritual and intellectual confusion into the city (more specifically, for introducing novel religious practices and corrupting the youth).

Also worth noting, however, is that Socrates lived the last days of a life that had brought him to complete intellectual uncertainty and a shameful death with triumphant composure, as though he had magnificently succeeded in all that he had attempted. At his trial, his defense was characterized, as his conversation always had been, by a calm but disconcerting irony. In prison, he refused to save his life by escaping (although this could readily have been arranged) because of a voice murmuring in his ears, "like the sound of the flute in the ears of the mystic," that told him that he thus would betray the laws under which he always had lived. He devoted his final hours to discussing whether there is life after death, apparently approaching the question with complete openness of mind; and at the very end, after "readily and cheerfully" drinking the hemlock, he calmed his weeping friends.[1] Socrates did not act like one who had been reduced, by thinking, to a state of total perplexity. His ignorance seemed to be the paradoxical sign of an awareness that was inexpressible but so

[1] These events are recounted in three works by Plato: the *Apology,* the *Crito,* and the *Phaedo.*

powerful that even the imminence of death did not affect his tranquillity.

We have no certain knowledge of Socrates's political outlook. He was probably as unwilling to identify himself with definite political principles as he was with principles of any other kind. But it is not difficult to see certain broad political ideals exemplified in his life. To begin with, his whole career was a moving enactment of freedom. He was ridiculed by his fellow citizens and threatened with exile and death by the government, but imperturbably continued to live and to speak according to the unutterable but irresistible imperatives that governed his whole mature life.

Further, although Socrates may have had elitist leanings, such as those manifest in the idea of the philosopher-king, enunciated by his follower Plato, his manner of life suggests a certain egalitarianism. He did not claim special authority for himself (beyond his mission of demonstrating the universal ignorance in which he shared) and was apparently willing to talk with anyone who was willing to talk with him. In one of the Platonic dialogues he is depicted as showing that significant knowledge can be elicited from an uneducated young slave.

Finally, Socrates was a thoroughly communal man. Loyalty to the very city-state that sentenced him to death kept him from escaping, and his stubborn questioning represented an indefeasible openness to communication.

Socrates displayed that difficult balance between personal independence and social responsibility, between uncertainty and the capacity for action, that may be called "civility." He was apparently interested in all ideas, and in this way unreservedly open; in his absence of fanaticism, he was tolerant and disengaged. Through this same openness, however, he was thoroughly engaged in what was for him the most serious of all tasks, the search for truth. Through a similar paradox, he was "ignorant," unable to pronounce finally on the truth or falsity of any idea presented to him; yet he was capable of rare decisiveness and courage in the performance of his civic functions, on one occasion risking death by defying, on grounds of illegality, an order from a governing clique.

Today we scarcely even aspire to such a stance. It is assumed that the test of one's political seriousness is determination to produce practical effects; impassioned and uncompromising action is widely respected. Yet history has been heedless of our demands. After almost two hundred years of seeking to command events, modern man is nearly overwhelmed with misfortune. Could it be that what is required, rather than ever intensifying assertiveness, is Socratic civility?

For most of us, doubt is unsettling, and we avoid serious discussion because we are afraid of doubt. Socrates seems to tell us that doubt is a source of health and hope, and that the confidence of a free and communal person is born, strangely, of uncertainty.

We are living today in a period of uncertainty, but it is an anxious and debilitating uncertainty, not the serene and luminous uncertainty of Socrates. As brought out in connection with Question 19 above, not only traditional religious faith, but even confidence in science, is weak. Vast multitudes of people crowding the earth have no clear and stable ideas as to what is real or how they ought to live. The spiritual situation could hardly be more ominous.

If the idea of humane uncertainty is valid, however, this situation is not hopeless, and we should not try totally to eradicate our doubts. They may be a pathway to understanding. When we try to replace our doubts with objective principles that cannot be shaken or destroyed, we turn aside from this pathway. In doing this, we may be turning aside not only from the possibility of deepened understanding but also from one another. So fundamental a diversion can lead to the greatest disasters. The totalitarianism and violence of our time result in some measure from the efforts of men to escape from uncertainty. Those who cannot live with doubt cannot live with human beings who are thoughtful and independent enough to be sources of doubt.

Thus, for the sake both of understanding and of community, we may hope that our age of anxious uncertainty does not give way to one of perfect certainty. The greatest achievement of political thinking today would not be to overcome our doubts but to help us live with them in a state of freedom and civility.

Index

Index

church-state relationship, 153
Cicero, 12
City of God, The (Augustine), 22
city-state, 25–26, 31, 43, 80, 92.
  See also polis
civil disobedience, 11–12
class, 66, 67, 70, 94, 137, 175; and
  inequality, 53–54; and unity,
  44–51. *See also* inequality, conventional
class conflict, 45–47; and liberalism,
  48–49
classical economists, 75
Cold War, 107
Communism, 5, 71, 92, 133; and
  class, 46, 49; and inequality, 53,
  58; and socialism, 141–142. *See
  also* China; Marx, Karl; Russia
Commuist Party, 94
Communist Revolution, 161
community, 18, 23, 40–41, 45, 68,
  104
Condorcet, Antoine-Nicolas de, 183
Confessions (Rousseau), 68
conservatism, 76; and class, 47–48;
  and estrangement, 28–29; and
  freedom, 116, 117–118; and liberty, 133; and nature of man,
  136–137; and rationalism, 33–34;
  and unity, 41
constitutionalism, 58, 107–121, 161
crime, 154–159
Critique of Pure Reason (Kant),
  122, 180
Crito, The (Plato), 198 n
cynicism, 55, 63

Dawson, Christopher, 84
death, 4–6, 59, 197
democracy, 47, 107; direct, 92–93,
  95–99; radical, 66; representative, 95–99; totalitarian, 111,

119. *See also* constitutionalism;
  political participation
dialectic, 184
Discourses, The (Machiavelli), 77
disintegration, 22, 23
divine right of kings, 84
Dostoevsky, Fyodor, 39, 135

economics, 45, 75, 140, 142
egalitarianism, 25, 31, 48, 59, 70,
  90, 199
Eichmann, Adolph, 10
elitism, 31, 61, 62, 63. *See also*
  inequality
England. *See* Great Britain
Epicurus, 80–82
epistemology, 121, 169
equality, 53–72; and alienation, 70;
  and estrangement, 67–71; and
  idealism, 55; and liberty, 135,
  136; and power, 73; and socio-
  economic status, 64–66
Establishment, 53, 63
estrangement, 21–51, 67, 76, 129,
  147; and inequality, 59, 68–72;
  nature of, 22–26; origins of, 26–
  29; and rationalism, 30–34; and
  religion, 34–40. *See also* alienation
evil, 28, 73–74
existentialism, 122, 181
Exodus (Old Testament), 156

Fascism, 23, 49, 133
Federalist Papers, 96
forms, doctrine of, 178–179
freedom, 5, 15, 87, 115–120, 135,
  137. *See also* liberty
free enterprise, 75, 139–145. *See
  also* capitalism; private property
French Revolution, 53, 58, 133,
  166, 167, 169, 170

Index

Index